# Beckoned by the

# KING

## AN INTIMATE VIEW OF PSALM 119

### Jeannie Pallett

BECKONED BY THE KING
© 2008 Jeannie Pallett

ISBN-10: 1-897373-17-1
ISBN-13: 978- 1-897373-17-0

Unless otherwise noted, all Scripture is taken from the NEW AMERICAN STANDARD BIBLE®, Copyright © 1960, 1962, 1963, 1968, 1971, 1972, 1973, 1975, 1977, 1995 by The Lockman Foundation. Used by permission.

Scripture quotations marked (AMP) are taken from the Amplified Bible, Copyright © 1954, 1958, 1962, 1964, 1965, 1987 by The Lockman Foundation. Used by permission.

Hebrew alphabet pictures and meanings can be found online at www.biblicalhebrew.com. Used by permission.

WORD ALIVE PRESS

Printed by Word Alive Press
131 Cordite Road, Winnipeg, MB  R3W 1S1
www.wordalivepress.ca

An expression of the heart of Father God inspiring, strengthening and encouraging believers to move deeper into his presence in spite of life's obstacles.

# Contents

# Foreword

It has been my privilege to read this book. I have known Jeannie for many years and have watched her grow into the woman of God she is today. She is a woman of integrity who has walked through many hills and valleys in her personal life. When Jeannie shared with me three years ago about this book on Psalm 119, I knew that she was the woman who could do it. Like David, she is a woman who follows after the heart of God. Like David, she is a woman of passion who is passionately in love with her Lord Jesus Christ. Like David, she is a woman who has walked through many years of pain and in those times she has cried out to her Lord for mercy and grace. As I am sitting here writing this foreword, I started snooping through Jeannie's Bible. In Psalm 94, Jeannie has underlined verse 19, which says: "In the multitude of my (anxious) thoughts within me, Your comforts cheer and delight my soul" (AMP). In Psalm 95, verses 6 and 7 it says: "O come, let us worship and bow down, let us kneel before the Lord our Maker (in reverent praise and supplication). For He is our God and we are the people of His pasture and the sheep of His hand." This exemplifies Jeannie's life and her relationship with her God. She trusts Him implicitly and worships Him completely with her life. I know that you will be blessed by the words written in this book, as I was. And I know that you will be blessed by the gift that Jeannie Pallett has given you through this book.

*Pastor Cathy Toupin*
*Calgary Christian Worship Centre Ministries*
*Calgary, AB*

# Preface

Based on each Hebrew letter of the alphabet found in Psalm 119, this work is intended to inspire, challenge and motivate the reader to a deeper place of intimacy as these eternal words of truth are contemplated and meditated upon.

*Beckoned by the King* will take you on a journey of joy as the heart of the Father is revealed and you connect with the God who has bound himself to his people by his passionate and unquenchable love and desire.

These pages are the result of experiencing the character shaping lessons of life and being willing to wait and not run from the prick of the sword as God has kept me in the fire. Many times it would have been much easier and far more comfortable to run, but early on he reminded me that, when I am in the refiner's fire, I am actually in the midst of his burning, passionate love, and his desire is to fashion me into a woman who more closely bears his image.

It is my prayer that in these pages you will hear the voice of the Lord speaking to your heart and begin to understand and experience for yourself the passion and fascination the Lord has with you.

I present this gift of love to you and pray that it will ignite a deeper passion in your heart to know the deep and intimate things of the Lord.

*With love,*
*Jeannie Pallett*
February 2007

# Acknowledgements

I owe heartfelt thanks to Bruce, my beloved husband and best friend, who has consistently shown me incredible love, incredible love, incredible love. Thank you for your infinite patience, which I know has been tested many times. Journeying with you and having our hearts knit together in love is truly partaking of the finest gifts of the King.

To those dear friends who have encouraged me in my walk with God, thank you. Your words of encouragement have been like nuggets of gold that I have treasured in my heart.

To the King, who has joined us to himself so we walk as one—all glory and honor is yours.

# THE KING'S VISIT

WOULD YOU BE ready if I came to your house today? Do you worry and wonder what I'd find?

If I came to your house today, would I find a place prepared for me, a place set aside where you draw away to be with me?

Of course, you know that I know just what I would find, what I would see and what atmosphere I would enter into. If I came to your house today I'd find a people occupied with what I have set before them to do. I'd find a people prepared and ready with willing and obedient hearts joyfully working as unto me regardless of their position or station upon this earth.

There are daily rituals in each of your lives, and in each of your lives I would find hearts in a posture of waiting. This pleases me and I will come.

*I will come* to you in your kitchens as you ponder my Holy Word; I will come to you in your vehicles as you set out to begin your days. I will come and take your hand that waits to be enclosed in mine that I might enclose you and enfold you in the strength of my presence.

If I came to your house today, would you stand in speechless wonder, would you lay prostrate at my feet? My presence would bring peace and I would overshadow you, all worldly thoughts to cease.

If I came to your place of work today I would find you working with heart attitudes that mirror my Word. I would find your hearts positioned at my feet, drinking of the Rivers of God.

I have no favorites among you; you are all my favorites and my heart is moved by love and throbs to hear you invite me into the days I have planned and prepared for you. My heart thrills to the sound of your voices, but even more, I am moved as I see your hearts positioned to wait upon me.

Rest assured I will come, for I know the deep longing within your hearts to be truly touched and transformed by me. I will give you new names that reflect my work in you and purposes for you.

*When I come* to you I will take you by the hand and say, "Come, my child, let us go to the place you have set aside for me." There we will sit and have sweet, satisfying fellowship as you behold my glory and my goodness and I unfold for you the secrets of my Word.

*The deep longing in your hearts will be met.* You will enter in and be swept farther into the deep waters of God.

Every physical, emotional and spiritual need will be met as deep calls to and is answered by deep.

As we sit in the secret place, my heart will know joy unspeakable as you carefully fashion your questions and responses. I will laugh with you as you realize I know them even before they are on your tongues! I love you so. Enjoy the peace of my presence even as I enjoy looking upon your waiting hearts. I will fill the empty places.

Sin will not reign in your bodies, for my grace is abounding towards you and has overtaken you. Together we will work through those areas you have difficulty with and together we will meet at the Cross. There my blood will flow; not in rivulets blocked by sin, but flowing unstopped and with mighty power to reach into the farthest corners of your hearts. In those areas that have been dark—not exposed to the Light that heals and restores—you will come to know health and wholeness.

In my strength and love you will find sustenance, nourishment for your souls and spirits as you walk through the days I have set before you. I see your hearts choosing life and blessing. I see your hearts waiting for a filling up, waiting to receive my presence.

Keep your minds alert; do well what I have put before you. Keep on positioning your hearts before me. Welcome one another as you would welcome me. Esteem one another highly. Love without partiality. Give expression and action to that love.

See me; hear me in the lives of others. Feed one another; share freely with one another the good things you receive from me. Don't be afraid to be vulnerable and share the lessons I teach you and the growth in your understanding as I take you through your times of difficulty and hardship. I am there with you.

All of you have been given giftings by me, all of you are loved equally and all of you are becoming one body as you walk in unity. Recognize those areas in your relationships that need the loose ends tucked in and recognize the things you need to discard. Leave them at the Cross.

Walk as one, using your gifts to edify and encourage, to comfort and instruct, to give wise counsel, to serve, to give, to administrate. Use these gifts wisely; use them with sincere love, always holding fast to that which is good. It is in the outflow that I flow through you and into others.

I have taken you by the hand, called you by your name: Beloved, Precious One, My Peculiar People. I am teaching you how to walk in step with me.

If I came to your house, your place of work today, I would say, "Fear not, Beloved One, you have found grace and favor in my eyes and today my presence—I AM—will overshadow you. Deep within you, a new life in me will be strengthened and girded up. My Word will gird you, wrapped around you and bearing you up in all ways.

Beloved, I have come to you by my Spirit, your waiting hearts are sensitive to his stirrings; move with him, follow his nudging. Keep on walking by faith, seeing with the eyes of your spirits; let those eyes remain clear and focused upon me. I am not hard to find and I have promised that if you seek me you will find me. You will be found by me to be a people with hearts that wait.

*I will come to your house*, for I, too, am earnestly waiting, expecting, looking and longing to be gracious to you. Even though I am seated on the Throne, I lift myself up in order to have mercy and show loving kindness to you. You who wait for me are a blessed people. As you expect and look and long for me, so shall you receive in your lives my victory, my favor, my love, my peace, my joy and my matchless, unbroken companionship. Truly you are people who have made your hearts a place I love to dwell.

## Response to the King's Visit

O Lord, Mighty King, it is in your awesome strength that my heart will be glad. The salvation that you have brought to my life causes me to greatly rejoice. I have joy unspeakable because of all that you have done for me.

I am greatly humbled by all that your laying down your life has brought to pass in my life. You look at me in the midst of all your children. Your eyes meet with mine and they pierce me to the core of my being; yet behold, they are sparkling with love! You find no fault with me, for you have perfected me in your love and grace.

Your mercy showers me with blessings. It is raining, not cats and dogs, but blessings, and each raindrop is bringing continual fertility within my heart as I become a tree of righteousness planted in the house of my Lord.

The deepest cry of my heart, the deepest longing of my soul, is to walk with you. Wherever you lead me, the path shall be one of righteousness, and the effects of righteousness are peace and joy. Again and again I shall rejoice in your gift of salvation.

The victory that you have attained for me, O King, is generous and abundant. How great is the love, Father, that you have stored up to pour out into the lives of each of your children. The portion is so generous it cannot be measured. It cannot compare with anything we know in the natural.

You have been holding my heart in your hands and you have breathed upon it. Through your breath you have deposited within my heart all your dreams, desires, hopes and plans for me—dreams and desires that you have held in your heart for me long before you saw my unformed substance in my mother's womb.

You have protected me, guided me and brought me into your courts. I stand before you, Lord and King of my heart, and humbly bow and lay myself at your feet. You reach your hand out to me; tenderly you raise me up and look with eyes burning with love into mine.

You touch my heart, purifying, perfecting and polishing me, and then your proclamation comes and I can stand only because your arms have enclosed me so that I am drawn ever closer to your heart. You have given to me the desires of my heart!

As your breath mingles with mine, you show me pictures of myself in different stages of life, in various postures of prayer, and I behold, in all circumstances, my King does not withhold from me the request of my lips. You are, I see, running to meet me. You are running with such grace and beauty even though you look overburdened by the bowl you are carrying that is heaped high with blessings of good things. And I realize for every prayer prayed the answer is in the bowl and for every prayer not prayed you are urging me to lift up my voice and ask of you—to petition my King so you can show yourself faithful.

As you play this picture within me, you change the feelings in my heart about prayer. You also show me that in the midst of fiery trials I am in the center of your will as you are making me and molding me by the fire, shaping me inwardly to be like you. Indeed, my King, you have placed a crown of fine gold upon my head, not so I would be highly esteemed in worldly standards, but to forever remind me of my place in your heart and in your kingdom.

I am reminded by my continual feeding upon your Word that I wear a crown of life and your Word is the mirror through which I have sight. I ask life of you and you give it to me by causing all that is not of you to fall away and be destroyed by fire. You bring forth eternal fruit in my life as I allow you to teach me all that I am in your eyes and how great your love is for me. The crown you give me serves to remind me of my identity.

You uncover for me the enemies of my soul and drive them out by your mighty right hand, and you further impart and excite within me your dreams and desires for my life.

Out of the abundance within my heart I freely give to others. I choose to consistently look to you to be the Lifter of my head. And even as I make that choice, my prayer is that none of the world's glitter and charm would catch my eye. The enticement may be real, but I see it pales in comparison to the glorious goodness you reveal to me.

You are, indeed, O Lord, the exceedingly bright Light in the world. In your presence is fullness of joy because all of the enemies of our souls have been driven out and utterly consumed in your fiery presence.

It is good, O Lord, to be afflicted, for it is then our attention is riveted on the divine work you are doing in our souls.

I exalt you, Lord; I bless you and thank you for not giving up on me. Thank you for your strength that you wrap around me like a blanket, a comforter. You cover, protect and nourish me, and it is from that place of strength, by grace, that I sing and praise your wonderful Name and the exceeding greatness of your power.

In my life, O Lord, be exalted. Be seen in me by others; be heard and known, O God, in my voice, in my words and through my touch. May the light of your life shine through this broken vessel.

 # ALEPH

Literal meaning is 'Ox' or 'Bull.'
Symbolic meaning is a picture of oxen ploughing.
***'Strength, leader, first.'***

## PSALM 119:1–8

[1] *How blessed are those whose way is blameless,*
*Who walk in the law of the Lord.*

[2] *How blessed are those who observe His testimonies,*
*Who seek Him with all their heart.*

[3] *They also do no unrighteousness;*
*They walk in His ways.*

[4] *You have ordained Your precepts,*
*That we should keep them diligently.*

[5] *Oh that my ways may be established*
*To keep Your statutes!*

[6] *Then I shall not be ashamed*
*When I look upon all Your commandments.*

[7] *I shall give thanks to You with uprightness of heart,*
*When I learn Your righteous judgments.*

[8] *I shall keep Your statutes;*
*Do not forsake me utterly*

WHAT ARE THE signposts of success and prosperity that mark us in our society and in the world we live in today?

In the book of Leviticus, oxen were to be the sacrifice of the rich. Oxen had great strength and were of much value and worth because they were able to sustain a very heavy workload.

The man Moses was chosen by God to fulfill a plan that caused him to be shaped by his need of prayer, intercession and intimacy with God. Growing up as the adopted son of Pharaoh, no pleasure or need was ever denied him. Material wealth was his as a son of the king.

Yet, in the wilderness of his life, Moses identified himself as a son of the Living God, stripped himself of his own desires and endeavored to walk in obedience to God, even though, like us, he missed the mark at times. His failures, like ours, drove him to his knees so that he might be yoked with God.

Through prayer, he plowed the land of the wilderness, making way for the grace of God. That grace also appeared in the life of Joshua, who was yoked to the heart of Moses as he sat, day after day, in the door of Moses' tent, observing him. It was as he sat watching in the place of waiting that Joshua (and Moses) learned how to be mighty in God. Joshua waited and listened as Moses prayed, his prayer life sensitizing both of them to the thoughts, feelings and purposes of God.

Listening, waiting and hearing meant having a heart set on obedience, being teachable and pliable in the hands of the Living God. This was the time priorities were set, and this was the time of determining that which was of greatest value.

The time that we give to pondering that which we hold in our hearts determines its value to us.

The decrees and laws that God spoke to Moses would have overridden all else and been like liquid fire burning in his heart. They would have been burning away the carnality of his own thoughts and passions in order for him to be consumed by the passions of God.

By waiting in the presence of God, we, like Moses, are lifted to a higher realm of walking out our earthly lives. Over and over, God bid him to come up the mountain, and over and over again, up Moses climbed. He was neither transported nor translated; he had to put one foot in front of the other, empowered and spurred on by a heart set on obedience—a heart that was yoked forever with the heart of Almighty God.

Moses had been learning that the tumultuous events occurring in his life were to teach him the reverence and fear of Almighty God; they were not to do him harm. Rather, they were, and are, to prove our hearts through tests and trials so that we can all say we have been through the fire and through the flood, experiencing the touch of neither.

Our walk with God is an example to many. The cry of our hearts must be, "Lord God, I want to be obedient to your Word—not only the commands that tickle my flesh and make me feel good, but also the ones I can tell will be long, boring and tedious in the undertaking. Lord God, you have a plan for me. You have set me in this place and I choose, because I love you, to obey you with all my strength—even if it takes all I can muster—for I know this is exactly what you require of me."

As we wait upon God, his yoke becomes lighter upon us, growing easier and more comfortable to walk with. We are learning patience and humility. God calls, we answer. We wait while God is silent. Our hearts ache with love for him, yet we are in his presence nonetheless. We are surrounded by his glory and goodness, and we drink deeply from the cup he gives us.

What mountain is God calling us to climb to meet with him? How does God want to sharpen us? If we are bows in his quiver, he expects us to be fit for his use.

The very cores of our beings are exposed to God and he wants to change and shape us by his hand. The stone tablets God wrote upon, etching his desires for us, were broken, and yet, is this not how he wants our hearts—in anguish and repentance to be broken in order for the healing hand of God to mend and knit us together with his heart? Our hearts will then beat with the strength of the steady rhythm of his love as we find rest beneath the shelter of his wings.

The goal of our faith is the salvation of our souls. As we persevere and push through the obstacles, we will see Purity and Consecration as beaming signposts on the Highway of Holiness. There we will walk, securely yoked to the Father and to our brethren in the faith as the fire of God's love is embraced and greater degrees of holiness and purity are brought forth in our lives.

He so desires for us to walk together.

Today we hear a Voice within the deep recesses of our hearts guiding us in the way we are to go, and we recognize the Holy Spirit because of his abiding presence within us. It is he who helps us in the way everlasting. He speaks truth to our hearts and leads us in the ways that are right. He makes obedience to the Father a pleasure, brings delight to our souls and causes our hearts to beat with the joy of his promptings. We become like a threefold cord—not easily broken—for we are living the truth of the Trinity's purpose. We are fulfilling a walk of love, for love is captured in our obedience just as love was captured in the obedience of Jesus as he made his way to the Cross.

When Jesus encourages us to obey his commandments, he is not holding out to us a list of difficult, unpleasant, unattainable things for us to accomplish—he is holding out to us the invitation to love, to be captured within his love and to live within the context of his love.

Our hearts will be pure, reveling in the promise of seeing God. As we see and comprehend our neediness, the Kingdom of Heaven is unveiled before us. The entrance of his Word brings light; it illuminates our darkness and makes clear that which we have not beforehand grasped. It opens our eyes, so that we might behold wondrous things, and we experience great delight in obeying his Word. Our faith and obedience begin to walk together, and our sanctified selves begin to lose their fragmentation as our souls begin their renewal process to delight in the things of the Spirit.

As our souls rejoice in God, our bodies follow, and one after the other we lay down those things that have no place in the Kingdom of God. God rules and we are his. He is the Great King, the High and Holy One. We are his servants, though he has deemed to call us friends.

Walking on the Highway of Holiness preserves spirit, soul and body as we commit to diligently guarding against anything unholy entering our eye gates or letting our thoughts run awry. Instead, we stay focused in our choice to love Jesus no matter what. He will keep us, and it is out of the Father's Keep that we must live. If our eyes are the windows to our souls, what are we subjecting our eyes to that is influencing our minds, wills and emotions? And if we are living in the Father's Keep, what does he have laid out for us to behold?

It is then that we turn from our own musings to give consideration to the imparted words of the Holy Spirit. He is present in the Father's Keep. As he draws close to us, he reaches out and touches our eyes, saying:

*See, now, how to demonstrate mercy, to walk humbly with the Lord.* Love has washed over your eyes that you might see how to show kindness and to love without partiality. Humility clothes you and my vision supersedes and transcends yours.

*Yes, here in the Father's Keep the ways are the way of holiness, purity, never-ending mercies and steadfast compassion.* All of these are yours as you rest in my embrace and allow my hands to shape you, fashion you and perfect you. You will be no longer fragmented but whole and in peace. People of integrity with the sanctified spirit, soul and body operating in unison—this is peace; this is the rest in the Father's Keep.

All I have laid out for you is yours. Eat and drink, be filled with righteousness and the fruits thereof. Drink from the fountain of purity. Let your ear receive the Word from my mouth; it is food to your spirit, sustaining your soul and strengthening your body.

Go forth in joy and peace; stay leaning against my everlasting arms. I will keep you from falling. I will cause you to stand in a place of purity; your feet will be securely planted upon the Highway of Holiness and joy and gladness will rain down upon you as showers of blessing from within the Father's Keep.

Lift up your heads, lift up your hands, for the old has passed away and the new has come. The joy of Jesus is within you. Everything he has, all of his qualities emanate and radiate from his life and surround you here in the Keep.

Joy is a safeguard for your souls, and here in the Father's Keep alone it is protected and keeps you strong. Your willing sacrifice of self is the highest and best offering you can bring, for it is then that we are yoked together and walk in perfect unity. Joined thus, we walk as one.

# ב BETH

Literal meaning is 'tent' or 'house.'
Symbolic meaning is that of a household.

## PSALM 119:9–16

[9]*How can a young man keep his way pure?*
   *By keeping it according to Your word.*

[10]*With all my heart I have sought You;*
   *Do not let me wander from Your commandments.*

[11]*Your word I have treasured in my heart,*
   *That I may not sin against You.*

[12]*Blessed are You, O Lord;*
   *Teach me Your statutes.*

[13]*With my lips I have told of*
   *All the ordinances of Your mouth.*

[14]*I have rejoiced in the way of Your testimonies,*
   *As much as in all riches.*

[15]*I will meditate on Your precepts*
   *And regard Your ways.*

[16]*I shall delight in Your statutes;*
   *I shall not forget Your word.*

I AM THE house of God; I am the place where he dwells.

Keeping God's Word is the foundation that keeps us secure. His Word spoken to us brings us into intimacy with him. We reach for it and it keeps us from sin. It brings wisdom into our hearts, giving us joy in our relationship with him and a contentment that keeps us seeking after the holiness of God. The holiness of God causes our lives to become examples of humility and purity, the essence of the holiness of God.

The desire to be like him spurs us to live within the confines of his statutes. Our ears become attentive to his Voice, and the purer our hearts are, the clearer our ears will hear, just as the more we keep his Word before our eyes, the more the eyes of our hearts will receive enlightenment. We then run in the way of his commands and do not wander from them. His Word is the treasure of our hearts and we are filled with a hunger that only he can satiate. Nothing else will satisfy, nothing else will complete us. God and God alone will build and fill our house with joy unspeakable and his majestic glory.

We cannot remain the same; therefore he enlarges us to hold him, purifies us to carry him and guides us so that we walk uprightly with the ability to stand steadfast and sure in his promises. Truly, it becomes no longer the flesh that rises up for appeasement but Christ who lives through us, and it is the completion of Christ that is shown forth through the lives we live in the flesh. He teaches us to have dominion over the nature of our flesh so that the Kingdom is seen and Kingdom principles are lived. We become the well-kept house of God, each room swept clean, nothing hidden, no secrets, everything open to his holy sight.

# Traveler's Treasures

I was waiting, baggage in hand, for Jesus to come when an elegant man passed by and then stopped to speak with me. He asked where I was headed and where I came from.

"I have traveled far," I replied, "and the Heavenly City is my destination. There have been many hurdles and many trials to overcome, and though I have overcome some, so often I find I am wearied by the weight of these suitcases I carry."

With a smile on his face, the passerby questioned me further about my travels. I told him I had wandered through the valleys, and in the midst of the vale of tears, found the weight had shifted in my bags. Though heavy, they were no longer as burdensome and, in fact, felt strangely lighter.

I had been many places, seen many things and my heart had ached as I felt the pain of others' burdens. I had shifted my own bags in order to help others carry their loads. During those times, I reflected, things were so much easier for me to carry. In fact, it seemed during those times that I carried nothing at all myself. As I looked down and gazed at the battered suitcases at my feet, I took the time to ponder the contents therein. I wondered what it was I had packed for this journey. This journey was so full of newness—how could anything I had before equip me or be of any use to my present travels?

As the man continued his steadfast gaze, something deep within my spirit was piqued. His gaze was bidding me to do something. Could it be, in the midst of this crowded place, that he was, of all things, wanting to see the contents of my beat-up old suitcases?

I asked quietly. He nodded his affirmation.

So I kneeled down at his feet, fingers shaking as I began to unlock the case, only to find it opened with ease. It opened, and much to my surprise, nothing was as it had been!

With enjoyment and laughter sparkling from his bright, clear eyes, he sat down with me. Reaching out to me with a heart of love ready to burst, he watched as I unpacked the most wondrous contents one by one.

The first item was a garment I had never seen before; it was incandescent, beautiful beyond description. He told me it was from the times of great mourning I experienced that led me down the path of repentance and found me at the Cross. He called it the Garment of Praise. I remembered that it was at the Cross that I lost the heaviness that had so often weighed me down and hindered me from having a heart of joy.

As I gently put my hand on the next garment, I saw that it was a covering for my heart marked "Joy"—it, too, shone brilliantly. Even in the dim light of the suitcase it seemed to pulsate with the steady rhythm of the Father's heart. Each beat was a word of love, giving strength and encouragement as I had wearied in my journey. I took it, handled it, and then the man placed it upon my heart and it seemed to slip through layers and layers of hardness, each melting away under the incredible strength of his joy. He reminded me how, in the difficult times of dreariness, his joy and strength was a special gift.

Next was fold after fold of incredibly transparent fabric and this, he told me, was to replace the various masks that I tended to wear when I passed through lands of dread. No longer would I need these masks as the love of God, the joy of Jesus and the confidence of the Holy Spirit would be mine completely. I would walk with transparency before God and men and there would be no duplicity within me. My heart would be singly focused, my mind set, and both would, in unison, be reaching only to love Jesus more and more. My whole being would be set on pilgrimage and my life would be radiating the shimmering beauty of Purity and Holiness.

He spoke: "I bid thee, follow me." I rose and followed him into the light, leaving a trail of glory behind us for others to follow.

In the years that followed as this man traveled beside me, he told me many secrets of his kingdom, and my level of intrigue was so high and my love for him so strong that I could not help but stay as close to him as possible as he taught me about being the dwelling place of God.

Great joy was mine as he walked with me and shared his thoughts with me. He taught me that holiness befits my heart, making it a place where he can abide in comfort and joy.

I am concerned about how this Mighty Friend feels, and I ever incline my ear to his Word, spoken to me always with my best interests in his mind. Everything I do and say hangs upon what the Father says, so I intently focus and keep my gaze fixed upon him.

There are many distractions that pop up as unexpectedly as a jack in the box, catching me by surprise. The Father, in his brilliance and empathy, uses these "jacks" to mature me, assuring me that he is my covering and there are no limits to how high I can rise because I am reaching for him.

My greatest desire is to have eyes for only him and not to care more about impressions made on man.

His words, "I bid thee, follow me," burn in my heart like fire. As I walk in the light of the Love that surrounds me, my heart recognizes his bidding is much broader than a simple geographical location. The geography also includes the ground in my heart; he wants to walk in places not yet traversed and, as always, the sheer joy of his presence will strengthen me in the journey.

As we walk, he tells me I am carrying his presence and the closer I come to him the closer my life will resemble his. Deep calls out for understanding and deep answers my heart with the knowledge that I must issue death to my self nature so that his glorious nature will reign. And even as the death issue is warranted, he reveals I must have dominion over my flesh and subdue its evil desires.

All things are open to his sight; his gaze penetrates to the deepest core of my being and I know without question that nothing in me will escape the fire. He leans close and speaks, "Is not my Word like a hammer, is not my Word like fire? (Jeremiah 23:29) I am the Carpenter and I am the Blacksmith and I blow on the coals and shatter the rock of men's hearts, giving them in return hearts of flesh that will seek me. In finding me they will love me."

Although this Friend so carefully and intricately knit me together in my mother's womb and loved me with an everlasting love, there were things about me he didn't particularly like, and these were the subject of another conversation. He said, "Learn of me, for I am lowly." With a wince I asked him to show me what those things were that displeased him and to teach me how to overcome them, for I knew that he had said, "Be perfect as I am perfect," and I longed so much to be just like him.

"Are you willing to bear my mark?" he asked, "Are you willing to allow the holy fire of my touch to brand you, marking you forever as my own peculiar child?" I knew his

Word would brand my heart and be seared into my mind. No longer would my conscience be seared by guilt-ridden thoughts and impure motives, but the fire brand would purify, refine and cleanse.

He had my full attention and complete liberty to do with me as he saw fit, and I asked him to please continue working his redemptive work in me. I chose to be as soft, pliable clay in his trustworthy, gentle hands.

He laughed, and the love from his eyes shone brightly, shooting like rays of light straight into my heart where from flowed all issues of life. He issued Life with his words as he quietly spoke.

Lay up my Word in your heart, Child; it will keep you from sin. Keep watch on yourself so that your life— your words, attitudes and behaviors—conform to my Word.

Learn of me, learn from me, and then, from your lips declare and recount all the teachings of my mouth. Let them be the rejoicing of your heart. The treasure that you have sought is found in my Word alone. Declare it, speak it forth.

*Keeping my Word is the foundation that will keep you secure.* It will keep you from sin as it brings wisdom to your heart. As you walk in wisdom, so shall your intimacy with me deepen and great contentment and peace will be yours.

# ג GIMEL

Gimel speaks of a camel.
*'Dependable, strong and reliable.'*

## PSALM 119:17–24

[17] *Deal bountifully with Your servant,*
  *That I may live and keep Your word.*

[18] *Open my eyes, that I may behold*
  *Wonderful things from Your law.*

[19] *I am a stranger in the earth;*
  *Do not hide Your commandments from me.*

[20] *My soul is crushed with longing*
  *After Your ordinances at all times.*

[21] *You rebuke the arrogant, the cursed,*
  *Who wander from Your commandments.*

[22] *Take away reproach and contempt from me,*
  *For I observe Your testimonies.*

[23] *Even though princes sit and talk against me,*
  *Your servant meditates on Your statutes.*

[24] *Your testimonies also are my delight;*
  *They are my counselors.*

THE WORD OF GOD is reliable. *It is strong*, dependable and trustworthy. *It is our only enduring strength* as well as the only unchanging constant we can forever depend upon.

The camel's ability to drink vast amounts of water sustains it on the long journeys it travels with its master. So, too, as we drink at the fountain of Life we are sustained for the task at hand.

*As we partake of the Water of Life*, a steady rhythm and joyful cadence comes into our lives and we begin to show forth the praises of God. Through our everyday lives, supernaturally lived, he is seen as dependable and mighty.

Laid out before us is a Rock; it is the Rock from which we drink. It is that which has been split open for the Waters of Life to gush forth and have entrance into our lives. There are steady streams of refreshing if we would but stay, if we *could* but stay. But like the camel on his master's duty, we, too, must rise when our Master arises and says, "Come; let us go from this place." With joy we stand, eager to be about the Master's bidding. The narrowness of the path before us serves to press us ever closer to the Master's side. He is a generous Master and has dealt to us out of his bounty of blessings.

Along the way he encourages us to choose blessing, so that we might live a life of fruitfulness and peace. What a difference we find in our lives as we obey him and walk in harmony with his Word! We become as finely tuned instruments perfectly sounding forth each note our owner plays.

Within the cores of our spirits we hear the Word spoken to us and our hearts hurry to ensconce it, meditating on it, resting in it and obeying the fullness of it. God wants us to find rest for our souls; he wants us to lay our burdens down for him to gladly pick up and carry.

*He so desires* that we find comfort in his presence and that we cease from our own labor to enter into his rest. We are one with him; therefore, what he is, so are we in this world, and this becomes experiential reality as his Word unfurls like a petal in the light of our hearts.

*God hears and answers our cry* for him to pour his water into us that we might drink and drink and drink and have life in abundance as we keep his Word. Oh, that he would open our eyes that we might behold wonderful things from his Word, things too lofty for our minds to understand but that we perceive deep within our spirits.

May we see with the eyes of faith all the precepts and ordinances he has laid out for his precious children to behold and be beholden to. May we find great refreshing as the precious Spirit of God pours himself into us as we open ourselves fully to receive him. Let everything contrary to this in our minds, wills and emotions be crushed so that we can wholly long to follow his commandments.

We will be recipients of rich blessing as we walk in humility, willing to bow low and bear reproach for following hard after the only one who can fully quench the thirsting in our souls. *As we bathe* in the presence of the Holy Spirit and welcome his cleansing by the washing of the Water of the Word, we shall rise up strong, victorious warriors who show forth in our lives rich qualities of reliability, consistency, strength and dependability.

That which is shown forth in the human life is received from the Divine Life within. He is the one strong and mighty whose Word is such that it is solidly depended upon, totally relied on and found to be our only source of truth and strength. His Word becomes the joy and delight of our hearts as it guides us and counsels us in the way everlasting. We are to welcome and receive it so that we are able to walk the path he has prepared for us.

The Word becomes, as it were, our mode of transportation to get where we are destined. Just as a camel's master leads him to drink before and along a journey, so our Divine Master holds out his Word for us to drink to prepare us for our journey into our destiny. That Word, as we travel, will go down into the deepest parts of us and bring the Water of Life to our souls.

We welcome and receive the imparted Word so that the implantation process of deeper life can begin. We become sensitive to the Master nudging us to draw aside and sit with him for awhile, to rest and be refreshed in preparation for a more treacherous climb that he knows is ahead.

He calls us to be willing to give all that we have, finding our sole delight in heavenly treasure. He asks us to give, not out of our discarded leftovers, but to choose our favorite, our very best, and give freely so that with whole and undivided hearts we walk in the Father's Kingdom.

♛

*I have many places to take you*, many sights for you to see. You will look at them and see, not with your natural eyes, nor even with the eyes of faith. You will see with supernatural vision, and in that level of seeing you will perceive my plans and my purposes for that situation.

In the places I am taking you, you will also have great wealth and treasure at your disposal. You have found the greatest wealth in obedience to me; the greatest treasure is the joy your obedience brings to my heart. Use that which is before you to feed the hungry, clothe the poor and heal the sick.

It is no longer time to lay up treasures on earth, but rather, it is time to fully release an empty heart to me so that I may fill it with gifts from my hands. For I know just where, just how, to lay each gift within your heart, each carefully and tenderly wrapped in love.

*When you give your heart completely to me*, I hold it here, in the palm of my hand. Everything there is open for my inspection and receives my stamp of approval. A heart that is undivided belongs to me.

A heart that still follows after accumulating wealth is not one that belongs completely to me, no matter how much I have enraptured you with my love. The road of truth can be a hard one in which to walk, but you will walk it with strength and dignity as you empty your heart of worldly gain and drink from the well of salvation.

That well has as its source the Heart of the Father. Drink there, Beloved, drink deeply so that the water of Life can course through every cell of your being, washing, cleansing, that Love may arise out of the darkness and cover you with the light of my glory.

There in that secret place shall I protect you, provide for you and reveal my secrets to you.

Upon your heart is a banner of victory; upon your heart is inlaid my Word. Go forth with sword in hand, with precision cutting away the works of darkness.

My glorious love will shine forth always as a beacon in the darkness. It shall never be quenched.

*So drink deeply, Beloved Child*; each drop gives Life, each drop brings forth greater light. Drink, Beloved, drink of the waters of purity, wisdom, righteousness and the knowledge of God.

Here at the well you are as low as you can be, but in my Kingdom I honor your desire and willingness to live a life of humility and to lay your life down before man to surrender fully to me.

*Did you know, Child, that humility enables you* to carry a greater measure because self empties out and I can pour in? Yes, and that is exactly what Jesus of Nazareth did. He emptied himself, took on the form of man, a bondservant, and humbled himself to the point of death on the cross.

*The fruit of that death and resurrected life is you*, as I have highly exalted him and bestowed on him that Name which is above every name, so that at the mere Name of Jesus, every knee will bow and every tongue shall confess that Jesus is Lord to the glory of God the Father.

*So come, Child*, come and lie low before me. Drink and see me with the eyes of your heart as I work in you, fashioning you and making you fit and useful for the Master's Kingdom work. It is my great pleasure to do thus.

*Hold fast to the Word of Life.* Hold fast to Truth and surely you shall be kept. Yes! Go forth with joy in your dependence upon my mighty Word. I shall not fail you or disappoint you. I shall rejoice over you and share my joy with you, thus strengthening you in the continuation of your journey. By my side and in my heart you shall ever be. My eye is upon you and shall ever guide you, my words shall ever encourage and keep you as they run like water, refreshing your soul.

# ד DALETH

The Hebrew picture is that of an open door
when looked at from up above.
It is indicative of decisions made from a higher perspective.

## PSALM 119:25–32

$^{25}$*My soul cleaves to the dust;*
*Revive me according to Your word.*

$^{26}$*I have told of my ways, and You have answered me;*
*Teach me Your statutes.*

$^{27}$*Make me understand the way of Your precepts,*
*So I will meditate on Your wonders.*

$^{28}$*My soul weeps because of grief;*
*Strengthen me according to Your word.*

$^{29}$*Remove the false way from me,*
*And graciously grant me Your law.*

$^{30}$*I have chosen the faithful way;*
*I have placed Your ordinances before me.*

$^{31}$*I cling to Your testimonies;*
*O Lord, do not put me to shame!*

$^{32}$*I shall run the way of Your commandments,*
*For You will enlarge my heart.*

WE CHOOSE DAILY what flavor our choices will have, what will rule our thoughts and attitudes. Our feelings and our emotions are determined by whether or not our hearts are willing to take the path of the Cross.

Our first decision is determined by our willingness to die, denying self and acknowledging the rightful longing of God to reign in our lives in every area. It is in places we have never been—places we don't know exist, places we don't want to go to, places that are dark and lonely—that God longs to flood his light.

He so desires to renew our minds by his Word so that our inner man is filled with light and an understanding that far surpasses our mere knowledge of him. He wants our knowing to become an experience of his multi-faceted character as he reveals himself to us in the different situations that we face.

The tactics of the enemy are subtle and sly and we can easily find ourselves at an altar of idolatry. Somewhere a thought expressed itself that would have been better to cast down and brought into captivity and replaced with a thought reflective of the Word of God. Somewhere indecision lay rampant. Somewhere a door was left open; somewhere a heart cries for what is pure and true and right.

Here stands Jesus with sword in hand; here stands Jesus at the door of each of our hearts.

He is whispering. Can you hear his words of love and kindness, his words reminding us of his strength and his honor? His whispered words of intimacy are meant for our ears alone and not for a stranger to overhear.

*As I entered through the door of your heart when first we met, so I stand at the door and knock, hoping for deeper access into your heart. The door is but a place of welcome.*

Will I receive a warm reception and invitation to walk deeper within the walls of your heart? Will you, in fact, allow me to tear down those walls so that your heart will, literally, be undivided?

Yes! The door of your heart is where your greatest decisions are made. The attitude of your heart will greatly influence what choice you decide upon. If your heart is open, it is like a shoe in the door; there I can whisper to you words of comfort and encouragement that will guide you into making decisions that are right.

When your mind and emotions are reeling with worldly heaviness, I will be the Lifter of your head. I shall cradle your head within my arms and with great tenderness look into your eyes—they are the windows of your soul and reveal much. I shall speak Light into the darkness there and revive you with my Word.

In telling me all the ways you have taken, you have felt your heaviness lift off. I have answered you. My commandment to you is a lamp that has great potential to bring light to your darkened heart's doorway.

Choose to have a heart that desires to understand my precepts, for understanding my teaching clears away the shadows and allows you to see the brightness of my light. From the glow within, your mind will become renewed; you will sorrow in repentance but be strengthened according to my Word. Godly sorrow leads to repentance. Repentance leads you into the way of truth and light where I am able to reveal things to you I would like to remove.

That removal leaves room for you to hold a greater degree of the glorious presence of God as you show forth a faithful heart that keeps my Word ever before you. Cling to my Word and you will never be put to shame.

We are one and we work together. When you determine in your heart and make a deliberate choice to turn your face to my face, we enter into deeper relationship. You are fully turned my way, fully looking into my face, intently listening, determined to stay and not to close the door.

We are engaged, and the engagement must take place in order for the consummation of our relationship to be enacted. You see, my commandments are like the lampstand. They enter into your eye gate, but it is as you grasp my concepts that the Light dawns in your soul. And when you open the door of your heart wider, thus giving to me free entrance, we are able to have access one with another.

In our unity, I am the Door that you enter for access to the Father's throne room. It is a place with form and dimension, color and sound, unceasing throbbing Life. Humility, holiness, purity, praise and worship pervade the atmosphere and the pervasion is so rich and true it becomes a part of who you are. It is a most awesome place where Life knows wholeness and completeness.

This place of worship and adoration is where your answers to prayer originate. They are full-bodied and will encompass the realities of your now with that which lies before you. Things that you can't see and couldn't possibly know the Father knows and the Father sees, and his all consuming love and desire to care and nurture you motivates his answers.

Because there are many rooms in my Father's house there are also many doors. Holiness in its perfection is the source of the awe that permeates life in this Kingdom. There is a door marked "Holiness unto the Lord." It is a door that easily swings open, although the path to it is long and hard to climb.

The testimonies of those who have opened this door and entered in reveal the climb was well worth the arduous effort given to it. Self has died and been buried. The man who arrives at this door no longer resembles the one who began the journey. This new man is clothed in my image.

Though the journey has been lengthy and wrought with difficulty—though it may seem that rods of iron have blocked the way—yet the Son of Righteousness has shone upon your path with ever increasing light.

Keep focused on me. When your eye is sound, your whole body will be full of light. Let your daily decisions be choices that are motivated by the Lord your God's heart and then all that enters into you will be pure and wholesome.

The choice to open your heart's door to my steady knocking will always belong to you. Everything I have for you is good, and when you choose to truly hear me teach you my ways, meditating on the wonders and mysteries of God, the false ways you have pondered and taken will drop into the dust and the door of your heart will swing wider open yet, welcoming me more fully.

This is what it means to have an eye that is sound. The eye of your heart will accurately perceive, giving you a sound and stable mind, fixed upon and renewed by my Word.

HE

Speaks of a window through which we see.

## PSALM 119:33–40

33 *Teach me, O Lord, the way of Your statutes,*
*And I shall observe it to the end.*

34 *Give me understanding, that I may observe Your law*
*And keep it with all my heart.*

35 *Make me walk in the path of Your commandments,*
*For I delight in it.*

36 *Incline my heart to Your testimonies*
*And not to dishonest gain.*

37 *Turn away my eyes from looking at vanity,*
*And revive me in Your ways.*

38 *Establish Your word to Your servant,*
*As that which produces reverence for You.*

39 *Turn away my reproach which I dread,*
*For Your ordinances are good.*

40 *Behold, I long for Your precepts;*
*Revive me through Your righteousness.*

INCARNATE WISDOM, ETERNAL love and trustworthy truth are but a few of the qualities Jesus pours into our lives.

Jesus always speaks the truth to us in love, not only because he is Love and will not speak to us out of any other motivation, but also because he knows it will help us to much more readily grasp the gravity of what he wants to impart to us and enable us to walk in.

The Scriptures declare that in him we live and breathe and have our being. It is important that we first draw close to Jesus and allow his influence to bear upon our activities and the way in which we go about doing them. His mark needs to be on our perspective and how we respond to life. Things that seem just beyond our grasp become more readily accessible as we learn that we cannot even begin to function as children of God unless we have bathed ourselves in his glorious presence. We need to allow the Lord to take us by the hand and lead us into the pool of water he has drawn and prepared for us and allow his tender ministrations to cleanse us completely.

Is this not a picture of the intimacy that Jesus desires to have with each one of us? Our sin is screamingly evident in his presence, but he does not berate or belittle us; his breath alone breathed into us brings forth beauty, changing the lives of his Beloved.

The landscape of our inner lives is painted by his brushstroke, creating a picture of perfection. Even as a base coat affects the clarity of the color that is evident to others, his wisdom, love and truth cover us under the colors he is applying through our experiences.

Love purifies our hearts and gives us a crystal clear window through which we have a higher and untainted perspective.

There is no condemnation in the love of God, only a convicting of sin with a compelling need to live in the Spirit.

We need to grow up and mature in him so that we are fixed and stable, experiencing the steadying joy of Jesus so that we are unswerving in our emotions. Our speech should always be seasoned with salt and comprised of words that are gracious and kind and showing forth patience and long suffering. As we mature, we will prize wisdom and our words will bring healing and life and blessing to the hearer. We will learn not to retaliate—but oh, how often is the reality just the opposite!

It is then that we long for the comfort of God, for him to somehow let us know that, in spite of our downfalls, we are indeed still growing. But how and when will we be able to grow past our shortcomings and respond rightly? What do we have to do to allow the Mighty Savior of our souls to bring us victory in this area?

Quietly, unmistakably, in his crystal clear voice we hear him speak, urging us to…

*Come up here. There is a spot I've saved just for you, my Precious One.* It's here in the Father's Keep and there is a place for you right by the window so you can look out and see all the things that are taking place.

Here you shall sit and be delighted as I teach you and give you understanding of my statutes. In your fidelity to me you will begin to see and make observations through my law. And you remember well that my greatest commandment is to love.

So your eyes are washed in the Fountain of Life. It is here that you begin to see and know and differentiate between wood, hay and stubble, and gold, silver and precious stones.

*Contend for excellence; contend for truth.* Contend to take hold of the love of God. It is as you hold and carry my love that the wood, hay and stubble of your life is burned off and my Word becomes established in your heart.

My Word will be very fruitful, producing reverential fear of me, and that, in turn, will produce wisdom in you. To walk with wisdom is to walk with me. I am Wisdom, I am Eternal Love and I will cause you to stand strong and steadfast.

*As you sit with me at the window,* you will find that your vision grows continually clearer. Your vision determines the perspective you have on life, and when you are standing with me, your perspective will be higher.

*Your eyes are the windows to your soul.* If your vision determines your perspective, then your vision also sees what you are looking for. The Law of Love is to look for the highest and best in another, and when your heart is ruled by love, you then have a perspective of excellence.

*Love is the way most excellent.* In the times when you cannot see me, remember that I have given you the Comforter. You long at times for my comfort, but I have given you the Holy Spirit to be your Continual Comforter. He is at the window with you too, and it is he who rubs the windowpane free of any smudge. It is he who causes clarity to come to your heart's eyes, and in time all of my children will learn to live and do all things through him.

*The Holy Spirit's presence is a canopy all around you.* Acknowledge his presence, welcome him, for he waits for you and so longs for you to feel loved and special. Everything that comes to you in life is filtered first through me.

*A deeper walk of maturity and faith that works by love will cause you to look through the window of the Father's Keep by first looking through the Holy Spirit.* He is your personal Comforter and Counselor and he will counsel and guide you with wisdom. Together you will walk.

Your heart will burn from his teaching and this will bring to pass in you a new level of refinement and purification. He will speak of love, show you the qualities of love and instruct you in how to appropriate them in daily life.

In times of difficulty, he will bring his refreshing Word back to the forefront of your mind and literally teach you how to love in those circumstances. And so, he also becomes your personal trainer, training you in righteousness and the putting off of the deeds of the flesh, teaching you and training you to live according to the dictates of the Spirit.

*Can you tell me—do you choose to take your place with me by the window?* Let your eyes weep because you see the worth in those people the world devalues. This place by the window with your name on it is a place of pain and discipline, but with the pain comes great gain, great joy and incredible love.

*Will you sit with me by the window, Beloved?* Will you turn your gaze fully upon me? Will you let love rise as an edifice, giving you sight that is pure? Love will give you strength to choose the highest and the best. Will you sit with me at the window, Beloved, and let me cover you in my love? Covered thus, your sight will be true and pure. Excellence finds a way.

ו       *VAV*

Vav resembles a hook or a nail and is a picture
of how our lives hang upon God's love for us.

## PSALM 119:41–48

*[41]May Your lovingkindnesses also come to me, O Lord,*
    *Your salvation according to Your word;*

*[42]So I will have an answer for him who reproaches me,*
    *For I trust in Your word.*

*[43]And do not take the word of truth utterly out of my mouth,*
    *For I wait for Your ordinances.*

*[44]So I will keep Your law continually,*
    *Forever and ever.*

*[45]And I will walk at liberty,*
    *For I seek Your precepts.*

*[46]I will also speak of Your testimonies before kings*
    *And shall not be ashamed.*

*[47]I shall delight in Your commandments,*
    *Which I love.*

*[48]And I shall lift up my hands to Your commandments,*
    *Which I love;*
    *And I will meditate on Your statutes.*

THE LOVING KINDNESS of God has come to us in the person of our Lord Jesus.

All of God's love, mercy and grace are embodied in Jesus, who was promised to us since the beginning of time, in order to daily deliver us from the dominion sin's hold has over us. We also were a promise of a gift to Him.

We know well what forms sin takes in our personal lives, and we know that we constantly struggle to resist sin. Our victory lies in focusing our gaze so that our hearts rest singularly upon the Lord Jesus.

The Lord promises us that, if we seek him wholeheartedly, we will find him. We will find the place where he dwells, and as we wait upon him in that secret place, he will begin to reveal himself to us and fashion our hearts after his image.

God is not a man that he should lie, and as we make it habitual to wait, we will experience the revealing of the goodness of God. That rich goodness is a facet of the faithfulness and benevolence of God. His character is revealed in the fact that his loving kindness towards us never ceases and every morning his mercy covers us afresh.

His Word tells us that we are seated with him in heavenly places. Where is he calling us to come when he beckons us to come higher?

Seated in the heavenly place, we begin to look around at the awesomeness of our surroundings. We live on earth in natural bodies, but the eyes of our hearts behold heavenly glories…

WE SEE A huge, dazzling door, and here we are beckoned to enter.

We do so, entering into another new dimension in our relationship with Jesus, who described himself as the Door. As soon as we step through we know that the mysteries of Heaven will begin to be unveiled to us.

The secret place is the Father's Keep, and we are invited to come fully in and be taught morning by morning by him. We sit with him in this special place and he anoints our eyes, covering them, and yet the covering only brings clarity to our sight. Our vision is brand new and we recognize the presence of the Holy Spirit as he teaches us to see through him. We sit and wait upon him and become skilled at seeing Kingdom activities through Kingdom eyes of love.

He directs us farther afield and takes us to a higher place. This is a place of deeper intimacy. To get here we have had to resist the cries of many who would hold us back, but it is Jesus who beckons us up and he is the one we have chosen above all else. On the way to the loftier height we experience many trials by fire, many tribulations and temptations, but each time we declare the Word of the Lord and experience overwhelming victory in the face of great odds. It is here that we know that our love and faith work together. It is here we experience the reality of the faithfulness of God.

And it is in this moment that God causes us to see something new.

It is an immense hook that covers the length, width, height and depth of God's love.

It is here that he stops with us and somehow we know that our entire lives hang upon this hook that symbolizes the love of God.

He asks us what we have learned through all the sights of the Kingdom that have been shown to us...

I ponder in my heart before I reply.

"I know your loving kindnesses have come to me, O Lord; you have brought salvation to my soul. My mind is in the continual process of renewal by your Word, my will seeks to do that which pleases you and my emotions are becoming balanced by the fruit of the Spirit.

"I am becoming more like you as I choose to take the more excellent way of love. I have been learning and experiencing the loving kindness you have for me. I have felt the weighty presence of it as it has come toward me and rested upon me. I have been, and will always be, learning to allow your loving kindness to control, inspire and nurture me.

"I trust you because you have shown yourself to be utterly faithful, completely worthy of trust. You strengthen me with your might by your indwelling presence as I am in the midst of the fire of God. You show me it is there that you burn the dross out of my life and enable me to rise from the fire as pure gold.

"Most importantly, you are causing my heart to be pure as gold. What you have taught me is that my emotions and words come forth from my heart, and I must endure the fire so that the purifying process results in my becoming a vessel you can fill with your glory.

"I have great confidence in you, O Lord, because I have been experiencing the freedom and liberty that your love has brought. Constantly, you enable me to be who you created me to be and my confidence in you determines and sets my emotions. The fruit of the Spirit is growing in me; my love for you, Father, is determining my actions, thus causing me to walk in those good things you have prepared for me. I am free to be me in Thee, O Lord!

"You are complex and magnificent, and yet, there is such simplicity in your wisdom. You are always in the process of giving to me; the more I find my joy and delight in you, the more you pour into my life. The joy, Jesus, is unspeakable. It is a glorious, glorious gift you have so freely and abundantly graced my inner life with.

"Your Word, when I speak it, always accomplishes the purposes for which you gave it—it is full of great and awesome power. My sanctified experiences have been good teachers, and I am fully persuaded that your Word will always prevail, the only sure Word that I can fully depend on.

"In fact, I can hang my life upon that hook in your Keep and rest completely, knowing I am held by you. You can turn me whichever way you want as I hang on that hook, for I have chosen to be turned and shaped by you.

"Our homes often have hooks that we hang our coats and hats upon, and here in my heavenly home there is a hook waiting for me to surrender my life in the natural that I might live the truth of your Word that reminds me that in Christ I live and breathe and have my being. Truly, your Word, O Lord, is established and is my resting place."

# ז ZAYIN

The Sword is a picture of aggressiveness.

## PSALM 119:49–56

⁴⁹*Remember the word to Your servant,*
    *In which You have made me hope.*

⁵⁰*This is my comfort in my affliction,*
    *That Your word has revived me.*

⁵¹*The arrogant utterly deride me,*
    *Yet I do not turn aside from Your law.*

⁵²*I have remembered Your ordinances from of old, O Lord,*
    *And comfort myself.*

⁵³*Burning indignation has seized me because of the wicked,*
    *Who forsake Your law.*

⁵⁴*Your statutes are my songs*
    *In the house of my pilgrimage.*

⁵⁵*O Lord, I remember Your name in the night,*
    *And keep Your law.*

⁵⁶*This has become mine,*
    *That I observe Your precepts.*

IN THE PLACE of surrender and submission to the fires of God, he teaches us how to wield the sword.

In the melting pot the purity of the gold is perfected. It is there that the strength of the steel is perfected as well.

The Son of God, the Word wrapped in flesh, was tried by fire and came forth glorious and highly exalted. Jesus was aggressive in his choice of obedience. His choice was to die; his choice was to endure the uncountable agonies of mankind—not just my own personal times of agonizing, which at times seem unbearable, but the accumulated agonies of mankind too vast to count.

The melting pot was his to embrace and he did not shrink back. He was expertly skilled in the use of a double edged sword, cutting away the forces and works of darkness. The flames of fire blazing on the sword rendered ineffective the efforts of the enemy to sway him from his purpose.

The Sword is the Word of God. Jesus spoke it and evil fled. He spoke with confidence, aggressively standing in his place as the Son of God, the Word made Flesh who, for a time, dwelt among humanity. He left us a legacy, an opportunity to ourselves learn the disciplines of obedience. His Word has not passed away; many times in history the hand of God has covered it and protected it so that today we would know who we are in Christ and learn to effectively use the Sword of the Lord with authority, knowing our position in him.

Our God is a consuming fire; we live a new life in him. We are in Christ, Christ is in God and therefore, we live our lives in the midst of a consuming fire.

The Lord God sees our faith. To him our faith has substance and measure, and our faith brings him pleasure. When our faith is tested, we learn to endure, and the result of endurance is a people of faith who are perfected and complete, lacking nothing.

Each of us has experienced "winters" or "cutting times" when God has been at work to bring forth his plans, purposes and a revelation of his Person to us. These have been our times on the threshing floor where he has been carving out of us a new man in his image. Our grain of wheat is good seed that has been dying in order for God to bring about fruitfulness.

When we choose to pick up the Sword, we, too, will render the enemy of our souls ineffective. The Sword will cut away the foreskins of our hearts. Self-doubt, fear, pride, disillusionment and disappointment will be challenged and they will not sway us from the plans and purposes God has put in our hearts.

In our times of affliction, as we remember and meditate on the Word of the Lord, the Sword in our hand is sharpened and hope rises. We rise up, standing taller in the light the wielding of our Sword has brought forth.

We hear a song in our spirits and give voice to a song of praise and wonder, for we have lifted high the Name of the Lord our God in our darkest night. We have been determined to live a life of obedience and have found that it has been as we used the Sword in our hand that hope and inspiration have risen up and a quiet confidence in God has settled upon our hearts.

We have seen the victories the Sword has brought to us and we are strengthened because the Lord of Hosts has made his counsel wonderful and his wisdom great. We are his to cover and protect, to nurture into mature sons and daughters.

Our roots are buried deep in him, and it is from this strongest place of security that we observe the battles raging around us. Our maturity has taught us to be lithe and active, our skills sharp through reason of use. We are skilled warriors, strong in the Lord and in the power of his might, standing firm, resisting the temptations and lusts of the world, recognizing the snares of the enemy and confident of the fit of the armor of God we wear. We can, therefore, stand steadfastly, and having done everything, we continue to stand firm.

Encouragement comes from Jesus, our Mighty Warrior:

I stood in meekness and humility and therein lay my greatest strength because I knew in my flesh I could do nothing but that for which the Father had empowered me. My boldness came from the strength of my humility.

The Father loves you even as he loves me, and when he sees you choose humility, he is there to lift you up and pour his grace upon you. I have known my place as the Son and I came before the Father as his child—not as one on a great and mighty mission too proud to serve or be needy, but knowing that my Father was always my source of strength and courage to see me through.

Blessed are the poor in spirit for they shall see God. I walked with him always; he gave to me the shield of his salvation and he protected and kept guard over my heart. His right hand constantly held me up, he endued me with power through the Holy Spirit and it has always been his gentleness and condescension that made me great. He girded me with strength for the battle and those who rose against me he subdued under me and caused them to bow down.

*Meekness marked my character*, and so it must mark yours to keep you from being marred by the enemy. As you bow down and lay aside and count as worthless your worldly treasures, you will begin to have sight that sees the treasures of my Kingdom. Let your heart be strengthened by my Grace, finding in me greater satisfaction and contentment than what the world offers.

The world offers the promise of battle and discouragement, disillusionment and failure. Come and stay with me and let me take you by the hand and teach you how to use the Sword with skill. I speak the Word, and the Sword of the Lord cuts through death, creates new life. It is sharper than any double edged sword because it has gone through the tempering fires of God.

As the dross is burned out, more and more of my Word will enter in. Amazing light will rest and grow within you, and from that place my Sword will grow sharper in you. Bring it forth in times of darkness and despair and see it gleam. See the cohorts of the enemy scatter as you lift it high. See their destruction as you land a piercing blow.

I have made your feet to be like hind's feet, able to stand upon high places. You will stand on the high places that have belonged to the enemy; with agility and grace you will tear them down. You will sing songs of victory throughout the dark hours of your nights.

You will walk a walk of obedience; you will feel the sharp prick of the Sword when you stray. That prick of love will keep you forever, for you will be inclined to walk the way of the straight and narrow.

Always remember, the lines have fallen for you in pleasant places. I hold and maintain your lot and have given you a good heritage. You are rich because I became poor, and all the treasures of the Kingdom of Heaven are for you. Let the greatest joy and delight and highest aim of your heart be that of seeking me and finding what I have stored up to bless you with. All that you can imagine—imagine, and I will do far beyond for you. You will aim at and hit the mark.

HETH

A picture of an enclosure, fence or hedge.

## PSALM 119:57–64

[57] The Lord is my portion;
    I have promised to keep Your words.

[58] I sought Your favor with all my heart;
    Be gracious to me according to Your word.

[59] I considered my ways
    And turned my feet to Your testimonies.

[60] I hastened and did not delay
    To keep Your commandments.

[61] The cords of the wicked have encircled me,
    But I have not forgotten Your law.

[62] At midnight I shall rise to give thanks to You
    Because of Your righteous ordinances.

[63] I am a companion of all those who fear You,
    And of those who keep Your precepts.

[64] The earth is full of Your lovingkindness, O Lord;
    Teach me Your statutes.

THE ENCLOSURE OF this hedge of protection is something we enter of our own will and accord. The opening into the enclosure also gives us the ability to leave whenever we desire, and nothing but ourselves keeps us there.

This Hebrew letter can also be likened to the opened arms of the Father, who is waiting to enclose us within his embrace of love. When we give ourselves to the strength of that embrace, the love poured into us brings about division that brings us into unity. We are separating ourselves from the worldly, weak, fleshly things of life and entering into captivity. We are saying, "Yes, Father, capture my heart," and in saying this we are recognizing that all things must change.

In warfare, cities are captured when their lines of defense are destroyed and broken through. At this point the city is wide open and completely vulnerable to the whims of the captor who can totally destroy it or rebuild as he sees fit. The spoils of that city belong to the captor. Moment by moment we choose who the captor of our souls will be, and when we allow the Word of God to define our lives, it becomes our boundary; it hedges us in and protects us, and within the boundaries of this hedge we are free.

The freedom of this boundary gives us the strength to be vulnerable. This vulnerability in turn shows us the truth about his strength being perfected in our individual weaknesses. When we decide to yield to him, our warring hearts will quiet as we realize that our own lines of defense will never hold, never bring about victory.

Each one of us are in warfare, engaging in many different activities, and each one of us lives with defenses, duplicity and deceit, wherein the end is destruction until we are willing to be captured.

To be captured by compassion is to allow ourselves to be held in the womb of the Father and be nurtured and nourished by him. It is to know that he sees all the days of our lives and he knows what our deepest need is and is fully willing to see it come to pass in our lives.

And yet, we must not struggle for position within the enclosure of his womb. We must not strive and kick against the goad, but rather, we are to rest as he feeds us, as his life nourishes and strengthens our weaknesses. He watches us and is waiting to see the image of his Son being formed in us.

It is the pure love of the Son that becomes our only defense, for he is our refuge, our shelter, our strong tower, our Deliverer.

This is truth—this is where our victories begin to take shape as his love is made perfect in us. He who loves and treasures the Word of God is not easily offended, and he who loves covers over and forgives an offense.

In taking the offensive there is no protection, for an offense in one's heart causes bitterness and jealousy and unrighteous judgments to lodge within, making the spoils of the heart the enemy's possession. We have entered into the enemy's territory of our own will and volition, taking things that do not belong to us, and we are caught holding the bag of tricks that have tripped us up. This dirty bag of tricks is what Jesus died for to free us from. Unforgiveness, guilt, shame and unrest all roll around in the bag, causing our hearts to be knotted with tension. Our hands are clenched around the drawstring of the bag until we see the light of love's truth before us and with great fervor and emotion we cry to the Father to take our hearts captive.

In this captivity, we are cleansed, forgiven and set free from the hold of the enemy. Compassion has seen that mercy is poured out over us, and the lifeblood of the Father brings us into unity with him. We are no longer standing with one foot in the enemy's camp and the other in the victor's camp, for we have learned that our Captor requires more than half-heartedness. He requires more than we can sometimes even give, for he requires our lives.

His promise to us is that if we are willing to lose our lives—to lose the emotions that have ruled our lives—we will find ourselves rising to higher lives of peace and joy un-speakable, joy unstoppable, joy that spills over and colours every part. He is life, he is joy and he is our Captor, for he has taken every one of our unrighteous emotions and transformed them. He has taken every aspect of our lives and poured his life and healing into every corner as we have come deeper into the enclosure of his protection and immersed ourselves in the safety of his womb.

Mercy triumphs over judgment. There is no longer a de-fensive or offensive line of demarcation, just simply the trail of blood from the cross that covers our lives and brings us into victory. Just as one soldier covers another in warfare, so the blood of Christ hides us as we claim its power and enter the enemy's camp and take back all that has been stolen from us. We have peace, love, joy, perseverance and endurance; we are rich in mercy, steeped in compassion and the heart of the Father beats strongly in us. We have now been clothed with dignity and righteousness and crowned with the victor's crown.

Come and enter into the joy and rest of the Lord. Come and enter into a land that is pleasant and peaceable. I surround you when you enter in; I am all-encompassing and offer to you my pledge of protection as you live within the boundaries of the hedge I have set. The lines have fallen for you in pleasant places and within those lines I support you.

I am your portion and I will help and support you in all your decision-making processes. You will learn my ways and what pleases me line by line, precept upon precept, here a little, there a little. Maturity comes to you as you allow me to teach you through your circumstances, and through those lessons you will grow up in the knowledge of God and the grace so freely given. You will learn to live in my domain and be stayed upon me.

As you live out your promise to me to keep my Word, so shall my grace, favor and blessing be given to you. My graciousness extended to you will far exceed your expectation. I will do exceedingly above and beyond all you can hope for or imagine, and my Word shall bear fruit in your life.

It pleases me when you give heed to your ways and make choices to set your feet to run in the path of my commands. My heart beats a little faster from the pleasure I receive from seeing you hasten to keep my commandments. There is no delay in your response, for you have learned that you and I cannot bear to be parted by sin and unrepentance.

My heart aches at any separation from my Beloved, and it is good when your heart longs for me and chooses to follow hard and close to me.

The snares of the wicked are always present, but you are experiencing the mighty strength of the cords of love that have bound us to one another. I hold you by the arms and teach you how to walk in union with me.

The words of my law are etched upon your heart— they center you and great is your peace and undisturbed composure as a result. The fruit and effect of righteousness is peace and joy, and both belong to you because of your commitment and choice to love.

*When you rise in the night because of your heart's pining* for me, my presence shall overshadow you and I will give you rest. I will speak words of life to your soul and refreshment will be yours in great measure. You will rise at the breaking of dawn and know that you have met with the Most High. I am your Companion, your Faithful Friend; I am wisdom and as you walk with me, you shall grow in wisdom. You shall accurately perceive the times and just as accurately walk out the truth I reveal to you. It will be my Word that defines who you are.

*You will walk rejoicing within the boundaries of the hedge* that is there to protect you. Within the boundaries you are free. Free to love, free to discover to the fullest extent who I have made you to be. Freed to walk in the plans and purposes I have for you, freed that you might live out of the Kingdom's treasuries.

Love for one another will be your only debt. With total confidence in my Word you shall take the Sword of the Lord and cut away all fear and doubt. I will inspire you to greatness and equip you with all things needed to fulfill what I have written in the Book of Life about each of your todays. I know what tomorrow brings; I am eternal and see into your heart now. *Today and Now are the hands that tick on my timepiece.* Now, I see you strong in the Lord and the power of my might. Now, I see you aggressively pushing away those things that reach out to you to try to snare you. Now, I see you making determined, definite deliberations that will result in praise and honor to my Name. Now, I see you seeking to find me to eat my words and drink the waters of the Spirit.

There is a River that flows from the Throne of the Most High, and you are in the midst of it. It is cleansing, changing and conditioning you. Now is the time of consecration to me. Now is the time to see the fullness of my loving kindness and now is the time to be taught the unfailing statutes of the Lord your God. Now is the time to walk wisely before me. I am your Portion, your Deliverer. I am sufficient for your times and you share in all I am and have for I have freely bequeathed it to you.

# TETH

**'Flexibility, shrewd, wisdom.'**

## PSALM 119:65–72

[65] You have dealt well with Your servant,
   O Lord, according to Your word.

[66] Teach me good discernment and knowledge,
   For I believe in Your commandments.

[67] Before I was afflicted I went astray,
   But now I keep Your word.

[68] You are good and do good;
   Teach me Your statutes.

[69] The arrogant have forged a lie against me;
   With all my heart I will observe Your precepts.

[70] Their heart is covered with fat,
   But I delight in Your law.

[71] It is good for me that I was afflicted,
   That I may learn Your statutes.

[72] The law of Your mouth is better to me
   Than thousands of gold and silver pieces.

THE LORD HAS given to each of his children a portion of land in which to dwell and he instructs us to keep busy with being good and faithful stewards of all that he has blessed us with. Of all that he has blessed us with we are to give back to God one tenth.

Our tithe is precious to the Father because it shows him that we have hearts that desire to please him and consider obedience a greater thing. As well, it shows him that we are willing to trust him and live by faith in the Word of God. Our desire culminates in the reality that we do, in fact and in deed, please God.

Our giving back of our tithe represents our selfless act of love towards the Father. It shows him that we will take steps toward being a people who are without mixture. When we hold back, he stays his hand of blessing toward us. Ease in every area of our lives comes when we are completely ready to say, "Your will, Father, not mine. I choose obedience to your revealed will and thank you that you will reveal yourself to me as Jehovah Jireh."

Indeed, we have a God whose eyes are never removed from us, seeing into the cores of our hearts and knowing intimately those whose hearts are completely his. He is always giving us his strength, whispering his thoughts into our hearts and ears, giving us his truth as a shield and buckler—a fortress to protect us from evil.

Grace has come to us through the Lord Jesus—he meets us in our desert places and wilderness experiences and touches our stony hearts so they become warm, soft and pliable, bearing good fruit. Our hearts become baskets woven with the experiences of life, brimming over with wisdom and flavorful fruit that incites a thirst in others.

When the "stuff" of life weaves its way toward us to throw us off course, let our confession of faith be that we are running purposely, with our eyes fixed and focused on the goal. We see Jesus clearly at the end posts, arms outstretched, and his cheer encourages us to run the race and run it well. He sees all the things that tend to trip us up along the way, and he sees us stubbornly holding onto things that don't belong to us.

In addition to the tithe, there are many other things we hang onto that belong to God: fear, pride, shame, guilt, anger, impatience, unkindness, selfishness and self-centeredness. In keeping hold of these things we are robbing God of delighting in his ownership of us.

We have been bought with the precious blood of Jesus. We are fully paid for and everything we are and have belongs to the one who paid the highest price. We no longer belong to ourselves; therefore all of our self nature must be handed over. The divine exchange benefits us, for we have had the righteousness of Jesus credited to our account.

Inasmuch as the enemy of our souls is shrewd and cunning in his attempts to poison us, we are called to be wiser still. We are to learn how to perceive, sensing in our spirits those things that have vitality, excellence and real value. It is vital to our spiritual health that we learn quickly and well the traps of the enemy, how and where he sets them and how to be diligent in stepping around them or, better still, casting them down in the Name of Jesus so they are brought to naught and do not come to fruition in our lives. The enemy's greatest desire is to trick us into thinking we are still bound in the strongholds and snares he set. The truth is we have been set free by the power of the mighty Name of Jesus, and appropriating that truth in our everyday lives means we do not allow ourselves to stay in sloughs of despondency.

When we feel woebegone, our born again nature must rise up and declare, "Woe! Be gone in the Name of Jesus; let joy arise in Jesus' Name." Walking in the authority and confidence of Jesus in greater measure comes with the fuller realization that Jesus reconciled us to God by his death and resurrection in order to present us as holy, faultless and irreproachable gifts to the Father.

Let us no longer walk in areas of darkness, compromise and confusion, but rather, press in toward the Light, being grounded, settled and steady in our faith walk. We have been taken from the kingdom of darkness, set free from the controls of the dominion of darkness and planted in the ground of the Kingdom of Love.

The precious love of God has borne the pain of all our sin. Because of love's bleeding heart, our sin is covered so that the Father's eyes see only the highest and best and most noble in us. Will we cling to love as he teaches our hearts good judgment, the wisdom of discernment and the patience to acquire knowledge? Will we cling to Love in our times of affliction? Our precious Jesus will be faithful to show his goodness and kindness towards us, enabling us to walk in those same qualities as we allow him to teach us through those affliction experiences.

Can you see the truth dawning in your heart? Can you see the light of his Word becoming brighter and brighter so it alone shines as a beacon in your heart? Is understanding now brightening your mind?

Come—come to a place in your walk where you are able to continually give thanks in times of affliction because you know that God is at work in you to purpose and do his will, his good pleasure. From the open hand of God will come to us his correction and discipline, and we must not shrink back from him. He will stir up issues in our lives simply to get our attention and help us recognize our greater need of him. We will see beyond ourselves to the greater purposes of God, knowing that he paid the penalty, the full redemption price for all our sin. May God help us to persevere in our "pressure cooker" situations. They are there not to drag us down, but to draw us ever closer. Don't respond or react to the taunts of the enemy, but listen for that still, small voice that is ever speaking to us, ever longing to be heard.

Come and return to the Lord your God. Let not despondency and despair over your sin keep you away. Grieve over your sin, rend your heart in repentance and know that I have torn in order to heal you. I have caused you to be stricken in order to bring healing.

Come, that you would begin to understand me and my ways; be zealous in your desire to know me. The more that you know and understand me, the more will you appreciate and cherish me. Your obedience then becomes a result of your love. My desire and my delight rise when I see you choose to love and do good.

Your tithes and your offerings are important acts in your relationship with me. I am pleased that you would trust me thus. To be a person without mixture will be your lifetime goal. As you take the axe to the root of self's unruly emotions, victory in these areas will be yours in greater measure. Never will self and spirit mix. Never can light and darkness abide together. Give me your unregenerate self; give me your heart, that my love fills it.

I will reveal myself when you seek me and turn from your sin. Be no longer an illegitimate owner of that which does not belong to you. None of your sinful ways rightfully belong to you anymore. My death cancelled them out. They are no longer yours to walk in, so step away from the old and begin to steadfastly walk in the newness of life I have created for you. Do it as an act of your will. Do it by faith. Choose the Spirit's fruit that brings life and blessing, joy and peace. Then your life will be crowned with love.

# ׳ YODH

Yodh resembles a closed hand or fist clenched to work.
Yodh is the only letter that is suspended in mid air.
Yodh is also the smallest letter and was used as the number ten.

## PSALM 119:73–80

[73] *Your hands made me and fashioned me;*
*Give me understanding, that I may learn Your*
*commandments.*

[74] *May those who fear You see me and be glad,*
*Because I wait for Your word.*

[75] *I know, O Lord, that Your judgments are righteous,*
*And that in faithfulness You have afflicted me.*

[76] *O may Your lovingkindness comfort me,*
*According to Your word to Your servant.*

[77] *May Your compassion come to me that I may live,*
*For Your law is my delight.*

[78] *May the arrogant be ashamed, for they subvert me with a*
*lie; But I shall meditate on Your precepts.*

[79] *May those who fear You turn to me,*
*Even those who know Your testimonies.*

[80] *May my heart be blameless in Your statutes,*
*So that I will not be ashamed.*

DEEP IN THE heart of the Father there lay a dream and a desire that he was shaping.

God Most High sought and longed to give expression and form to that which was rising ever higher in his heart. Everything that we would ever have need of and find enjoyment in he began to make reality long before we even existed.

As he planned, he held the dream, hidden within the enclosure of his hands. At the appointed time he began to speak out of the abundance in his heart. How he wanted to proclaim his faithfulness and love to all the generations that were yet to come!

Wherever he was in his high and holy place, perusing emptiness, he also saw it filled with beauty and abundance, color and light, form and rhythm, life and laughter. He could hear the song of joy the morning stars sang, and he knew the measurements of the foundation of the earth. He commanded the morning light to shine and darkness to fall at evening; he caused the dawn to know its place and knew where the dwelling place of light and darkness was. He created the wind and the thunderbolt and storehouses for snow and hail; he brought rain and he brought life to vegetation. He is the Maker of the morning dew and frost and ice and water; the galaxies, constellations, clouds and lightening are his, as are the rainbows and sundogs, for they all flowed forth from the power in his hands.

Abundance without measure, creativity beyond comprehension—this is the work of God. Ten times God said, "Let there be," and there was, and there has been, and there will be until he speaks again to change what he ordained. The tender, loving hands of God have carefully fashioned each of us, forming us into his masterpieces and commissioning us to work, to receive just wages and to give back to him the firstfruits, or ten percent of our earnings.

In our harried, hectic, hurried and worried world, we wonder sometimes at the logic of his command. We worry and wonder whether or not we will have enough, we question and balk at what God has asked of us. Our hearts hold concerns and care, showing that our focus has shifted and we are no longer settled, steadfast and secure in our knowledge of our Creator Father.

If we would choose to look beyond ourselves to his provisional promises—if we would position ourselves to see the love glowing in his eyes as he watches us work and walk—we would win in our struggle to stand against sin and self. The glow of love would draw us ever closer, ever higher. We would bow and, as his servants, be quick to do whatever he tells us to do. Our actions might be weak and watery but our hearts' motives would be pure and he would take our offering and pour out of it the choicest wine.

When we choose to tithe, obey him and learn to work with him, our lives become marked by joy as we delight in his law. God pours back into our finances as well as every aspect of our lives that we involve him in. Our "doing" is infused with the strength and power of God. Our decision to wait upon God results in receiving his faithfulness, loving kindness, compassion and joy.

Meditating on the precepts of God brings forth the light of revelation to our hearts.

We should never put our treasures ahead of giving to our King. He has promised that he will supply all of our needs and that he will do exceedingly above and beyond all that we could ever hope for or imagine. To cement these promises, he tells us that they are "Yes and Amen" and that God is not a man that he should lie; he is willing to swear to his own hurt and he does not change!

The work of my hands is good. I formed you and fashioned you in the womb of your mother, but even before you were conceived I knew all about you. I knew the time of your birth and appointed a time for your death and planned and prepared for you all along the road of your life. I saw that the work of my hands was good, and it was pleasing to me. I excelled in my workmanship; you are a work of perfection.

Nothing is missing or forgotten. You have been intricately woven together in my image and I see in you what I am.

There is no darkness in me at all, and I see you as a child of light and truth and love. Walk securely in the knowledge of my thoughts and feelings toward you and then know that they are compounded in my heart a trillion million times. My loving thoughts toward you are too vast for you to count.

Obeying my law of love and giving heed to my voice results in great peace and rest in your soul. Freedom is yours to walk in. Skip and dance with joy, Beloved, let laughter and songs burst forth from your lips. Your walk with me is a walk of glory and joy, let the light of my glory within you shine, shine, shine.

GOD'S HANDS COMMUNICATED his love as he made us, putting every part of us together to function as he saw fit.

As it is true in the natural, so it is in the spirit. His hands have carefully crafted us, placing within us personality traits that, when yielded to the Spirit, would cause us to be fit together for the Master Creator's use, aptly formed for his purposes and desires.

Even as he knit us together in the wombs of our mothers, so he knit us with his love to form the Body of Christ. As Jesus is the exact expression of the Father, so is the body to reflect the unity the Son has with the Father.

As individuals within the Body, each of us is to reflect the nature of Jesus. As we yield our minds, emotions and wills and surrender our hands, feet and mouths, so will we be filled with a greater measure of the Spirit of God. Our beings will become infused by his mightiness and that which we put our hands to will be fused by the strength and mighty power of God that flows from his hands that are ever resting upon us.

He is ever fashioning our inward, wayward beings to be stayed upon Jesus. As we focus ourselves upon Jesus and wait in his presence, we wait with expectancy to receive, for the Lord himself is waiting for us. He is expecting us, his heart is yearning and looking for us and, in fact, he rises to pour out his mercies upon us morning by morning. Jesus gives to us an abundance of joy and delight when we choose to set our hands to the plow and not look back.

When we choose to do battle against the kingdom of darkness, he promises us the victory because of the finished work of Jesus. His steadfast love comforts us and inspires us to tarry for him and wait for his Word.

We are his perfect workmanship, enclosed and hidden within his mighty hands. There we are kept safe while doing the works he asks of us; security is ours, knowing that the might and power of God shall prevail.

## *Elohim* – Majestic, Glorious Creator.

We are recreated in Christ Jesus to do the work he long ago prepared for us to do. Not only has he prepared the work, but also our hearts and minds, fashioning our whole beings so that we might walk in his works being whole, complete and free, lacking no good thing to do that which he sets before us to accomplish.

My plans and purposes for your life shall prevail, and they shall do so because you are in my care and within the enclosure of my hands. My eye is ever upon you and I am continually leading you and guiding you in the way that is right for you. I am ever drawing you closer to my heart.

The nearer you come to laying your head upon my breast, the more you will understand that submission is an act of love, not just a choice that you will to make. Love yields, love surrenders. Love seeks to obey. Love motivated my creation of you and Love forms my image and nature in you. Love is the greatest gift I have given. Love has also made the greatest sacrifice, but the result is you, my beloved children, in whom I receive great pleasure.

# כ KAPH

Picture of a hand that is open; the hollow of the hand.

## PSALM 119:81–88

[81] *My soul languishes for Your salvation;*
*I wait for Your word.*

[82] *My eyes fail with longing for Your word,*
*While I say, "When will You comfort me?"*

[83] *Though I have become like a wineskin in the smoke,*
*I do not forget Your statutes.*

[84] *How many are the days of Your servant?*
*When will You execute judgment on those who*
*persecute me?*

[85] *The arrogant have dug pits for me,*
*men who are not in accord with Your law.*

[86] *All Your commandments are faithful;*
*They have persecuted me with a lie; help me!*

[87] *They almost destroyed me on earth,*
*But as for me, I did not forsake Your precepts.*

[88] *Revive me according to Your lovingkindness,*
*So that I may keep the testimony of Your mouth.*

SINCE THE DAYS of old, a pattern has been established for the children of God—we are to live out our days kept in the hollow of God's hand.

We are always set before him, for we are the apple of his eye, the masterpieces of his creation. He finds great pleasure and satisfaction *in* us, and loves to give *to* us.

And yet, as the shriveled and smudged wineskin becomes so from the smoke of the fire it hangs above, so often we, too, bear the mark of affliction before we receive the blessing. Our souls become faint and wearied by longing for God's salvation, but hope is birthed from our renewed spirits, rising up strong because it is settled upon God.

In each of our lives we go through experiences that cause us to make choices either for or against God. His Word tells us that he has made each day a day to rejoice. Each sunset giving way to a new sunrise gives us fresh opportunities for obedience in small things.

Rejoice. This is a fact that is to rule our emotions. Without questioning the relevance or reasons, we are simply to rejoice.

But when the days come that threaten to topple the tranquility of the lives we enjoy, what gives us balance and stabilizes our hearts? The Word of God that we have hidden in our hearts rises to quiet the straying thoughts in our heads that threaten to take us way off course. The apostle Peter tells us to rejoice and be exceedingly glad when we face trials and hardships.

Our hearts will be able to rejoice when we make the choice to worship our unchanging God of mercy and might, compassion and companionship. His friendship, his loving touch, his spoken words, his whispered encouragement and comfort all come to mean so much more than anything outside of him can bring to us. He is worthy of our praise and adoration, worthy of our worship and exultation regardless and in spite of anything we see in the natural areas of our life.

Over and over again his Word proclaims that he has goodness stored up for those who love and trust him. God has such a precious steadfast love for us. He takes great pleasure in the prosperity of his children, and we are prosperous when we wait for him and hope in his mercy and unfailing loving kindness.

The deepest core of our beings waits earnestly and expectantly for the Lord, for he has promised to be our Help and our Shield. We are one with him, and because of our unity our hearts are joined and in him our hearts rejoice. Let us never grow weary in waiting upon him, for his mercy and loving kindness is upon us in proportion to our waiting and hoping for him.

We can rejoice in our afflictions, for they cause us to look for, hope for and wait upon our God. In the good times of our lives, let us guard against complacency and let God arise so that his enemies are scattered. Let God arise in our souls so that we can look about and see his salvation taking place.

He is even now encamped round about us; he is even now instructing us in righteousness and truth so that we are living to bring pleasure to the heart of the one who loves us so.

When difficulties come into our lives, instead of being anxious and ultimately slain by them, let faith well up from deep within, knowing without doubt that this is not a trouble unto death, but rather, a Call to Arms. Trouble is a call to unity within my own tent so that my arms can be linked to another, free to hold on because I am holding nothing but the power of God in my life.

It is a Call to Arms within the body—to weep with those who weep and to rejoice with those who rejoice; to cover the back of a fellow servant, to intercede, to strengthen and do our part in protecting them.

The Call to Arms is the Call to Unity. Jesus longs for us to be one as he and the Father are one. Our unity comes at the cost of obedience, letting go of pride and allowing God to establish us through difficult circumstances so we can sing of his great love and how he has turned our mourning into dancing. For how else shall we dance with joy and hopeful exultation unless we have known despair? How shall we have beauty for ashes, save for the fire of refinement?

We must learn, like Jesus, submission and obedience with joy, for in that way we enter deeper into sonship. We must learn, in the times of trial, to bow down before the Father and not buckle under imagined strain and stress, for the Father himself has told us to cast all of our cares upon his shoulders. He will shoulder the load for us.

It is the natural reaction of our flesh to fear, to fabricate lies and to fall into the sin of fretting. When our hearts are one with the Father, we will see that Jesus had unity in his spirit, soul and body—all were set on obedience to his Father. When what was happening caused him to despair before going to the Cross, he laid his life before the Father and his Father gave him hope by showing him a picture of each one of us.

Jesus had friends who were fishermen, and so it was a very graphic picture to them when he told them to cast their burdens upon him. Casting requires purpose, enthusiastic determination, strength and aim. The nets were heavy, as are our cares, and it took all their strength to pick up the nets and throw them out to the sea.

In casting a line we aim and throw and, as in our prayers, are very specific in our intent. The Bible tells us to come boldly before the throne of grace, and so, when we enter his holy place, our hearts are already laid bare. We are emptied of cares that weigh us down and hold our hearts; we are no longer divided, for we have cast our cares upon Jesus.

The cares of life bog us down in so many ways that are deceptive and deceitful—we find there is so much to love more than Jesus, so many better things to do than to pray and learn his Word, so many other things to occupy our time rather than spending it with the King. These are the things that must be emptied from our hearts in order for us to be pure and without division. It is equally all of these things which we must cast upon the Lord.

We come meekly and with humility, but we also come with confidence, having learned the art of casting. Casting is not quietly laying something at the feet of Jesus, hoping that he will have taken it. Casting is a "heave-ho" action that requires us first to be anchored.

In the natural, if we have cast into the water, the net or line tends to float back towards us and whatever debris is around will also be attached. We have the most sure Word of God as an anchor for our souls. His Word says he answers before we even call and that the earth is his footstool. God is, as it were, reclining upon his throne, his feet resting upon the earth; nothing fazes him or catches him by surprise. What catches us by surprise is the fact that he has already taken care of our needs, already supplied that which was lacking. We don't know just how very much God loves us and wants us free to just love him in return. Every time our minds become cluttered, a housecleaning must be done and we must ensure that our anchor is solidly held by the power of God's Word.

"Fear not, be of good courage." These are not just words of encouragement but commands by which we are to live our daily lives. Our lives are lived moment by moment, one action at a time, and we must live them specifically and focused on the only thing that brings life, light and clarity to our souls.

Jesus can be seen, if you look, with arms wide open without a worry or care, and yet, as the one who carries us, his intercession is constant and sure.

When the disciples had been out fishing all night without catching anything, they were discouraged. When Jesus appeared and told them to cast their nets out on the right side of the boat, he was also instructing them to do away with their weary discouragement and obey him. Jesus had seen them toiling unsuccessfully, and as he sat on the beach cooking a breakfast of fish for them, his heart longed for the time when all men would walk in steadfast trust and obedient faith.

Our sins have been covered, gone forever in the sea of God's forgiveness and forgetfulness. If we would learn to heave and cast with enthusiasm our cares upon him, our aim would become sure to never miss the mark. Right at this moment, in our time, in our world, God is perfecting all those things that concern us. God is fashioning and forming the things that whittle away at our peace into something that will ultimately bring him praise, honor and glory.

# ל LAMED

This is a picture of an Ox goad; it prods the oxen with a sharp point so they do not stop in the middle of plowing. It is also shaped as a sickle in order to clean the plow.

## PSALM 119:89–96

[89] *Forever, O Lord,*
  *Your word is settled in heaven.*

[90] *Your faithfulness continues throughout all generations;*
  *You established the earth, and it stands.*

[91] *They stand this day according to Your ordinances,*
  *For all things are Your servants.*

[92] *If Your law had not been my delight,*
  *Then I would have perished in my affliction.*

[93] *I will never forget Your precepts,*
  *For by them You have revived me.*

[94] *I am Yours, save me;*
  *For I have sought Your precepts.*

[95] *The wicked wait for me to destroy me;*
  *I shall diligently consider Your testimonies.*

[96] *I have seen a limit to all perfection;*
  *Your commandment is exceedingly broad.*

BEASTS OF BURDEN were trained by men to do work that was long and tedious. Under the hot glare of the sun there must have been times when their physical limitations were strained, and yet, they were equally yoked with another from whom a quiet, inward strength and resolve to finish the task could be drawn.

This picture offers much to us today if we allow the eyes of our hearts to see how God yokes us with other believers. The Blood makes us all one, but we are yoked only to a specific number in our sphere of influence and God has some specific requirements of us.

He goes before us in our journey through life calling our names, inviting us to come closer into his presence. He wants for us to be gathered with him in the light rather than standing in the shadows because we are unsure of his reception. In the center of the pool of light surrounding him we see him with outstretched arms singing to us, *"I love you, I love you, I love you,"* and before he takes a breath to sing another stanza we run and jump into those strong, secure outstretched arms.

We are his, he has betrothed us to himself and he rejoices over us with another love song. Any doubt, questions or fear we had are gone, replaced by an inward knowing that forever his Word is settled in heaven and he is utterly trustworthy.

We see through the eyes of faith that all throughout the generational lines his faithfulness continued even when we, his Beloved, turned our backs and hardened our hearts. Amongst the generations there always a remnant who knew it was hard to kick against the goad and one to another they began to share the love of their Father and encourage each other in their faith.

Their faith was working by love and the grace of God strengthened and encouraged them as he perfected their love. They saw the establishment of all that had been created and saw that everything was servant to him, the Creator. It was plain to see that they themselves had been created in order to fit into the Creator's grand design, and as they sought to learn of him from his Holy Word and inquire what his purposes for them might be, his words began to become etched upon their hearts and from this great joy was derived.

A special invitation had been given to them to enter into intimate communion with the Creator Father through the Son's love gift of himself. The response was to be in kind— to offer one's self to him, to be at his beck and call and to become totally consumed by his love, with his fiery word burning all dross from one's heart.

The power of love consumes our enemies, drives away all negativity and fleshly attitudes and strengthens our resolve to choose him regardless of the hardships to our flesh. We are his and he who is Forever Faithful will save us.

In seeking the Heavenly Father's heart he shows us the wiles of the enemy and fortifies us to his onslaughts. All the more diligently we learn to apply his Word and see the victory he attains for us. We learn that our walk with the Father is one wrought with difficulty and challenge, but the promise to us is that we are overcomers and more than conquerors. Therefore, we can embrace with great joy and expectation the afflictions that come.

There is a limit to worldly perfection, and not only are there limits, the perfection is also a facade, it is false. The love of God is that which is perfect and remains forever. The love of God is the goad that prods us, its sharp point zeroing in on our area of need. The Blood, shed for love's sake, cleanses us, reaching into the farthest and darkest corners of our hearts.

⚜

When the land is dry and you feel like you are kicking up dust, remember it is me tilling and preparing the ground of your heart for the planting of new seed. Healthy harvests come from healthy seed planted in healthy soil.

*Will you yield your heart* to my sickle and plow? Will you allow yourself to endure the momentary pain that results in the sharing of my glory?

I desire to sharpen you in your walk and the choices you make. Righteousness is yours; because of Jesus' trade at Calvary, you wear a robe of righteousness and I see you and consider you thus.

However, integrity and purity are choices you make daily; they are qualities seeped in the supernatural and those qualities are what cause you to have a higher walk. Walk with the wise—have a closer walk with me. I will enable you to do that which is difficult and encourage you all the while. You will come to the place of welcoming my chastening as your heart fully seeks my bidding and the fullness of your eagerness to please me grows.

# MEM

Fluid like water, has grace and beauty.

## PSALM 119:97–104

<sup>97</sup>*O how I love Your law!*
*It is my meditation all the day.*

<sup>98</sup>*Your commandments make me wiser than my enemies,*
*For they are ever mine.*

<sup>99</sup>*I have more insight than all my teachers,*
*For Your testimonies are my meditation.*

<sup>100</sup>*I understand more than the aged,*
*Because I have observed Your precepts.*

<sup>101</sup>*I have restrained my feet from every evil way,*
*That I may keep Your word.*

<sup>102</sup>*I have not turned aside from Your ordinances,*
*For You Yourself have taught me.*

<sup>103</sup>*How sweet are Your words to my taste!*
*Yes, sweeter than honey to my mouth!*

<sup>104</sup>*From Your precepts I get understanding;*
*Therefore I hate every false way.*

GOD IS FOREVER faithful to pour the water of his Word into us, causing us to be…

Reaching for the prize that lays in the upward call of
 Jesus
Straining forward to that which lies ahead
Pressing in toward the goal.

Onward, upward
Flying in the wind of God's breath
Soaring, rising up on eagle's wings
Flowing in the current of the Spirit

As a leaf flows in the current of the river
Flying or flowing, fetters freed,
But it's more than a leaf floating that I see…
It's an entire tree with its full root system intact and
 freed from the earth
And it is pure.

The roots are moving with exhilaration in the new
 freedom the river's current provides
The tree surges forward…
Reaching, straining, pressing in…

Does the River speak?
Yes! The River speaks.

It speaks so loudly all else is drowned out
But we must travel upriver to hear its voice.
Long before we reach the banks, the rushing, roaring
 sound of many waters reaches our ears.

…We stand at the bank of decision…

Our lives are like that tree
Standing tall and proud

With grace and beauty patterned year after year by its
   own seed.

The pull of the river is strong
The earth's forces desire to hold us back
The waters sparkle with life
They dance in freedom
Calling, beckoning us to come
To immerse ourselves, to join with others
In the free flow dance with Life
Pure, untainted.

There are roots that hold us back,
Roots of pride, insecurity, inferiority, rejection
Facades that slip, revealing glimpses of truth
They are bitter waters of which we do not wish to
   drink.

But the pull of the River is strong
The waters sparkle with Life
They dance in freedom
Calling, beckoning us to come
To immerse ourselves in the pure water of Life.

We stand on the riverbank
Lifting one foot and then the other
Only to find our root system so deep we are unable to
   plunge in as our hearts so desire.
Our hearts see ourselves immersed in the sparkling
   river,
Our eyes of faith behold ourselves being swept
In the current of the Spirit's flow.
The roots are holding us back
And we step away from the riverbank
Shame and embarrassment sweep over us
We want to run through the forest

Hide ourselves, standing tall and proud with the other
  trees
Whose grace and beauty are patterned
Year after year by their own seed.


Through the tumult of our racing hearts
The sound of footsteps in the forest reaches our ears.
Our heads are lifted
Our eyes behold a Mighty Lumberjack
One such as we have never dreamed.
He stands before us with strength and such ruggedness
  that we tremble.
The more we look upon him
We see an unmatched grace, and unfathomable beauty
A gentleness no strength could match.


He reaches out, knowing our hearts' cry for freedom
He stretches forth his arms
His hands touch us
The fire is burning within our trunk and the fire of his
  touch travels down,
Travels down, travels down
Farther and farther the heat burns
His arms wrap around us for we can no longer stand
  on our own
There is no strength in us; our imperfect balance is
  forever gone
And yet, we do not fall crashing to the ground
We are lifted,
    higher,
    higher, higher
Forever gazing into the eyes of the Lumberjack.

The fire is still burning in the deepest core of our being
Flames of fire are licking that which we have so long
Hidden and protected.
The roots are burned.

That which we thought would be so bitter tasting
Too painful to endure
Has been done as we have been captured by the Love
   of our Lumberjack's gaze.

His love has washed over us as the fire has burned
He carries us high above and we see a place where once
   we stood.
It is not a charred, empty hole in the forest at all
   but a place he has touched by his Beauty.
His Beauty has stood in that place
It is forever transformed.

Flowers grow nearby providing beautiful scent to the
   passerby,
Nectar for the birds as they fly unfettered, free and
   careless in the care of God.
We see mighty tree trunks
Stripped bare and flowing in the river's current
Leaping over the rocks,
   bouncing with sheer delight upon the river's waves.
No branches get hung up along the riverbank
It is streamlined;
the fire has burned off all the protective bark
Now it is bare,
   glistening in the sunlight and sparkling waters of
   love.

This is our goal
Freedom is our prize
This becomes our aspiration, our inspiration, our
   desperation
And we must forget what lies behind.
"I want to dance in the River with You, Lord"
   becomes the loudest cry of our hearts.

And so you shall, my treasure and my great delight. And so you shall, for your willingness to make the journey makes it easier for you to see it accomplished in your life.

It is written that the vision is for an appointed time and the time in your life is now. Enter into my River of Delight. You will become as the water; fluid, flowing with grace and beauty. Fluid and flowing, unhindered, unhampered.

You have asked me for the grace to grow in godly character and godly attributes. As you step into and plunge into the River, my grace is freely and abundantly given. It is yours. I have given you the grace to die so that Christ will be formed completely in you. I have given you the grace to die that you may live the abundant life I have promised you.

For, you see, the continual cry of my heart is "Come!" My continual desire is to pour my very best into your life. I stand here at the riverbank and am heard calling by all who desire to enter into the deeper waters. Deep is calling and being answered by deep. Let the waters swell and swirl and rise around you.

I Am the River of Life; immerse yourself and find me faithful. Immerse yourself and find me true. Be free, unfettered, dancing in the River with me. Enjoy the rich blessings of my love. Taste and see how good I am. Far sweeter are my words to you than honey in your mouth. This is my River of Delight and Great Joy! And so it shall be, as you see it in the Spirit, so shall it be in the natural, for the just live by faith and look at what is unseen. As it is in heaven so shall it be on earth.

# נ NUN

Likened to concentration.

## PSALM 119:105–112

[105] *Your word is a lamp to my feet*
*And a light to my path.*

[106] *I have sworn and I will confirm it,*
*That I will keep Your righteous ordinances.*

[107] *I am exceedingly afflicted;*
*Revive me, O Lord, according to Your word.*

[108] *O accept the freewill offerings of my mouth, O Lord,*
*And teach me Your ordinances.*

[109] *My life is continually in my hand,*
*Yet I do not forget Your law.*

[110] *The wicked have laid a snare for me,*
*Yet I have not gone astray from Your precepts.*

[111] *I have inherited Your testimonies forever,*
*For they are the joy of my heart.*

[112] *I have inclined my heart to perform Your statutes*
*Forever, even to the end.*

To stand in righteousness and walk in integrity, we must learn to wield the sword of truth and give heed to the shadows and darkness the light brings forth.

The tightrope of Truth is where we tread. The Highway of Holiness is a road raised up from the boardwalks of the world, up from where the glitter of trinkets catch the eye and the voices of those selling the wares of the world reach our ears.

Eyes and ears filled with lust cause hearts to become dull to the clear, pure voice of the Spirit, and we begin to lose our focus—concentration ceases, commitment to the Word of the King wavers. However, his steadfast love causes mercy and grace to flow out and touch the core of the heart that grows cold, fanning into flame the flickering fire and smoldering embers. Light shines into the darkness of our lives and suddenly we can see the paths we are to take.

There is a time of transitioning ourselves from the broad way to the Highway, a time of putting away the nature and desires of the old man and learning to become skilled in the putting on of the new man, walking adeptly with the full armor of God and clear focus.

Having learned the ways of God, let us determine in our hearts that we will keep them. There is one who walks forever with us, sticking closer than a brother, continually interceding for us and holding out to us the Lamp of Truth.

If we were to walk through our days consistently having our inner eye illuminated with the Light of the World, the essence of our lives would be confirmed by the love that motivates our faith and actions. We would have a walk of faithfulness and truth as we set the ordinances of God before the eyes of our hearts.

In times of affliction we would not flinch from the fire. Revival in our hearts comes as the Lord revives us according to his Word; purity is birthed as we learn the art of offering our sacrifices of praise. Grace flows freely and we easily escape the snares set by the wicked because the Law of Love is etched upon our hearts and no matter the test or temptation, we do not stray in our hearts as we have fully embraced the presence of Jesus with us.

We are eager and willing to walk out the precepts he has set forth for us to live with liberty, joy and freedom. We are no longer torn between two masters—there is only one lover of our souls and his bountiful love is forever entreating us to do that which is right.

It is liberating when we no longer cry out for his grace and mercy to cover us but, instead, live out of the fullness of the Holy Spirit within us. Purity then brings forth unity as we have learned to live being empowered and emboldened by the Spirit's holiness.

We flow with him with grace and beauty, doing his bidding, answering his beckoning. We have reckoned ourselves dead to sin and fully alive in Christ. Childish ways are put behind us; we step up to the plate of maturity, recognizing our places as sons and daughters in the Kingdom of God. We think, speak and act differently than before. We are clothed in love and humility and everything about us filters and flows through them.

Our flesh and our souls harmonize with our spirits and this unity also serves as our protection. We have been consistent in our concentration to be fully persuaded by the precepts of our Father.

As we run our race, pressing on and pressing in, we begin, through perseverance, to lay hold of the eternal things that Christ Jesus has already attained for us. We run the race, not having eyes flitting about and arms flailing, but rather, with tunnel vision, keeping our eyes on the goal and knowing that gaining the prize will cost us discomfort to our flesh.

Maturity and fruitfulness walk together, having had as constant companions Grace and Knowledge. Grace enables us when we need to experience the sufficiency of the Almighty, and Knowledge is the foundation Wisdom and Righteousness build upon. The one who is all knowing has prepared and established a path for us and shown us how to walk upon it.

The question is eternal. Are we willing to lose our lives in order for them to be preserved?

Jesus said in Matthew 19:24 "It is easier for a camel to squeeze through the eye of the needle than it is for a rich man to enter the Kingdom of God." It is time to draw closer to the Lord and ask him to press closer into us so that we feel his squeeze and the effect of his closeness is seen in our lives. Our inner man receives a cleansing and shines forth concentrated and pure.

We have need, great need of setting ourselves under his mighty hand to be molded and shaped, yes, but also to set, so that we become firm, faithful to the ways of God because our natures have been transformed and we are rising up in our new lives in Christ.

The freedom Jesus bought for us was for a purpose and it is this: that we learn to stand fast, cleaving to him and no longer allowing sin to be victorious in our lives. Let truth reign supreme in our minds, his Word so purging our thoughts that naught but his mind is in us.

Allow his Word to be the bait that captures you, his love to be the hook upon which your life is held. Learn to walk in his ways. Learn to trust him. Learn to lean into him and feel the weightiness of his presence. Let him set you as a precious jewel as in the breastplate of the High Priest. Forever he holds you close to his heart; forever he is reminded of you as his shoulders bear your weight. Great and mighty is the Lord Almighty and nothing is too big for him. Neither is there anything too small that he cannot see.

# SAMECH

Likened to the fulcrum or balance point
of a lever or teeter totter.

## PSALM 119:113–120

113 *I hate those who are double-minded,*
   *But I love Your law.*

114 *You are my hiding place and my shield;*
   *I wait for Your word.*

115 *Depart from me, evildoers,*
   *That I may observe the commandments of my God.*

116 *Sustain me according to Your word, that I may live;*
   *And do not let me be ashamed of my hope.*

117 *Uphold me that I may be safe,*
   *That I may have regard for Your statutes continually.*

118 *You have rejected all those who wander from Your*
   *statutes,*
   *For their deceitfulness is useless.*

119 *You have removed all the wicked of the earth like dross;*
   *Therefore I love Your testimonies.*

120 *My flesh trembles for fear of You,*
   *And I am afraid of Your judgments.*

In the Old Testament, when men shared stories of their past, their memories held pictures of a path marked by stones signifying the lessons they learned and how God helped them on their way.

These stone markers became like leverage points on the charts of their hearts so that when the elders relayed the accounts of the past to others, the story of God's faithfulness rose high above the mere retelling of the events. The eternal lessons of God took priority over the hardships of their past. They were a people set free to hope in the plans and purposes of the God of Abraham, Isaac and Jacob.

He became alive to them, for he is a living God who inspires a living faith.

Men of wisdom dwelled in the land and many inclined their ears to their words and set their hearts toward walking in the knowledge of God that was revealed to them. As they walked, they chose to put their trust in the Lord, receiving the eternal truths, knowing the certainty of the Word of Truth. They received words of excellence, counsel and truth—words that changed the way they lived, motivated their behaviors and molded and shaped their attitudes.

In our lives there is a spectrum that colors how we act and speak and see and hear. On one end there is an eternal weight of glory and on the other is the natural air of despondency and apathy towards the things of God. The fulcrum is in place but the weights need to be made even. We are exhorted to put off the old nature—to no longer be double minded and to wholeheartedly love the law of God. It is not the regulations and rules that amount to legalism but the righteous, holy standards of God that bring freedom and balance.

The Law of the Lord brings stability and balance into our minds. Our way of thinking is balanced evenly and we do not swing to the left or the right because the very core of our being is centered and fixed on Jesus, the one who came to fulfill the law. That desire to fulfill every jot and tittle of what was written about him, to be a Son well pleasing to his Father, became Christ's protection, his shield and defense against those things that warred against his flesh. In choosing to be that wholly obedient and pleasing Son, he also chose to experience great suffering that not only brought him great glory but also gave him the ability to have empathy with us in our time of need.

It is that same Word that we are to hide in our hearts. The Law of God encourages us toward the actions God expects us to do. As we are faithful to take his Word, the Bread we are to live by, into our hearts, God will be faithful to infuse his life into us.

This infusion causes us to enter into the all-consuming fire that he is, even as he sets his fire into our hearts. The fire of God frees us as he purifies us and captures us as we feel the steady, exhilarating balance and rhythm of the song of passionate love.

He cries to us and calls us:

Come. Come let me be your refuge and shield. Come, for I am faithful and true. I am the Living Hope, I am the Word made flesh. I AM. Put your hope and trust in me.

*Run to me and I will enable you to keep my Word because first, I keep you.* I keep you under the shelter of my wings, I keep you in my heart and I keep you in my love. I keep you and watch over your every move; my eye is ever upon you. I keep you in order to sustain you and bring fullness of life to you as you walk through lands of plenty and worlds at war. Your heart shall be balanced. I keep you so you are able to stand strong and secure in your day of trouble.

In your day of deliverance I find you keeping my laws and decrees, meditating upon my Word. The Word hidden and written on your heart keeps you, hides and protects and sustains you as I keep you in the refining fire that purges away the dross in your life.

Every need you will ever have is abundantly met in me, for I am the faithful keeper of your heart and soul. My blood was the price I paid for you—I own you and you are no longer your own. I keep you in the center of my love, and there in that place of deep, abiding love, my hands mold and shape you so that in every area of your life you are centered and balanced. I strip away those things that bring about unsteadiness in your walk and I wipe away those things that are an encumbrance and weigh you down.

*Know in the pain of the weight and the stripping* that I am perfecting you so that you are well able to walk with a full and just measure. All that you have is from me; all that is within you is from me. Remember that your present suffering is not worth being compared to the glory that will be revealed in you. Wait upon me, therefore, with eager expectation, for you shall not be ashamed of your hope in me.

# AYIN

Likened to a fountain of water.

## PSALM 119:121–128

<sup></sup>121 *I have done justice and righteousness;*
*Do not leave me to my oppressors.*

122 *Be surety for Your servant for good;*
*Do not let the arrogant oppress me.*

123 *My eyes fail with longing for Your salvation*
*And for Your righteous word.*

124 *Deal with Your servant according to Your loving-*
*kindness*
*And teach me Your statutes.*

125 *I am Your servant; give me understanding,*
*That I may know Your testimonies.*

126 *It is time for the Lord to act,*
*For they have broken Your law.*

127 *Therefore I love Your commandments*
*Above gold, yes, above fine gold.*

128 *Therefore I esteem right all Your precepts concerning*
*everything,*
*I hate every false way.*

I AM YOUR child, Father, and I live knowing you are the All-Seeing One. You see my past, my present, my future and, as the eternal rock of ages, you see it now. Time for you is always now and I have learned this by seeing how you answer before I even call.

You know the depth of my need, the fulfillment of every desire. You have exchanged my heart of stone for a heart of flesh and the heart that you have given me is full of godly desires. I have heard the proclamation of justice and righteousness resounding in the land and have stirred myself up to seek your face, touch your heart, hear your voice and see the tenderness that marks your ways. I am overwhelmed by your outpouring of love.

Your love washes over me like a fountain and I can but stay in the midst of it. In the midst of you, partaking of the meat and drink that you give me, I find balanced rhythm to my life. I am no longer yielding to the bait the enemy dangles before me, for my gaze has become set upon things eternal. I am focused on the goal and the way I see, when I look through eyes of faith, so truly determines the perspective I have on life.

You fill my heart with faith and teach me how to view circumstances through the eyes of my heart. The tricks of the oppressor are clear to me and your sweet voice guiding me is clearer still.

I can hear the excitement in your voice as your hand rests upon me. I yield to your slight pressure for I have chosen submission to my King. I turn only to look more clearly upon you and I see your eyes sparkling with joy at my eager obedience and desire to be led by you.

In the fire I have learned your faithfulness. Your truth burns in my belly, the dross of my life is removed in the furnace of affliction. I have stayed myself upon you, moving only in response to your call to come, to come nearer still and immerse myself in the love of the Father. This has become the focused goal of my heart, the purpose that drives my life.

All the walls I fearfully built for my own protection have been swept away by the washing of the water of your Word. You have spoken to me and called me your darling Beloved, and I run to you. Your love alone has readied me, steadies me to meet the love in your gaze as you look at me. I know that I am transparent before you—I can hide nothing—yet all you see is beauty.

When I am afflicted with trouble, I behold Your goodness; when the tyranny of the enemy threatens to oppress me, you are my surety, my promise, my guarantor for goodness. Surely I have learned firsthand that when I am seeking you and choosing your ways of righteousness, even when trouble comes to me, you deftly cause the situations to work out for my good.

There are times when my eyes feel they may fail from longing for your salvation, but I have seen over and over again that your salvation, your lifting up, always comes at just the right time. You show me mercy. You teach me your statutes. You share your heart with me.

And I know it is time to enter into an even deeper relationship with you, to walk moment by moment allowing you to lead in every one of life's transactions. Your salvation has, indeed, come to me, and I must always choose the way that is higher and harder.

The way of holiness will see me triumphing over all the enemies of my soul. So pure and beautiful will truth become that nothing will move me away. You beautify me with your salvation and your joy in me gives me cause to rejoice.

The righteous promise is you, Jesus, and you are the Word made flesh. You have come to me; your Word is true and faithful, a reflection of your character.

Would you teach me discernment, to see with the eyes of a faith-filled heart when I am unable to see physically? Would you so impact my heart with a deep understanding of your ways, your principles, your unchanging laws? Would you then deal with me, O God, disciplining me when I break your law?"

<hr/>

My discipline shall indeed come to you and your heart shall break and you shall weep over the rending of your heart. You will know great grief and sorrow as you see your sinful ways, ways that you tried to cover up, allowing compromise to tear your heart asunder. Compromise is devious, evil and subtle, and you must stay within the wall I have built for your protection.

I have laid the foundation in your life. Build your house upon the Rock, but be a co-laborer with me. Let me tend to you, lifting rubble from your heart until it shines as pure gold in the dazzling sunlight.

Yes! You shall walk on streets of gold here in Heaven, but your earthly walk shall be a walk of fiery love and everything you do shall be done in and through love. You in me and I in you—together as one we shall partake of the pleasures of love. So come, take my yoke upon your shoulders. Learn to live out of the fullness of the Holy Spirit within you and then you shall not be unduly affected by the tyranny of the enemy of your soul.

You shall look for and find rest for your soul as you see my salvation. Your ears will listen for and hear my Word spoken to you and I will break open my loving kindness and gentleness and pour it over you. You will learn humility in honoring and esteeming others, and through this decision I will further reveal my character. Your heart shall become that of a son or daughter in my house, and the heart that receives understanding of my ways shall blossom like a rose in the desert.

*No more shall the land be dry and barren, for it shall be saturated by my fountain of living water.* You shall see it and behold my pleasure. Through the law of love that rules in your heart, you endeavor to keep my commands. This costly sacrifice pleases my heart for my eyes see that faith has risen in your heart.

# pey

**'Open mouth.'**

## PSALM 119:129–136

<sup>129</sup>*Your testimonies are wonderful;*
*Therefore my soul observes them.*

<sup>130</sup>*The unfolding of Your words gives light;*
*It gives understanding to the simple.*

<sup>131</sup>*I opened my mouth wide and panted,*
*For I longed for Your commandments.*

<sup>132</sup>*Turn to me and be gracious to me,*
*After Your manner with those who love Your name.*

<sup>133</sup>*Establish my footsteps in Your word,*
*And do not let any iniquity have dominion over me.*

<sup>134</sup>*Redeem me from the oppression of man,*
*That I may keep Your precepts.*

<sup>135</sup>*Make Your face shine upon Your servant,*
*And teach me Your statutes.*

<sup>136</sup>*My eyes shed streams of water,*
*Because they do not keep Your law.*

THERE ARE MANY places we travel throughout life, many times we have opportunity to compromise and many occasions to harden our hearts.

Our Father is longing for a people soft and tender, yet with a determination of steel—a  people who will rise up and proclaim the wonderful testimonies of the Lord. These proclamations will result from knowing his incredible love and desire for us.

This is not a passive assertion or a casual acceptance, but rather, a legal and passionate betrothal, a covenant made by him with you and me and sealed with his shed blood. He is life itself to us and with great fervor we each stand and say, "Oh Lord, Your testimonies are wonderful. I have searched for them to write them on my heart in order that I might live them."

The words the Lord speaks to us are the testimonies that cause us to have undivided hearts of love. When our hearts are pining after his loveliness, then we will obey with unswerving affection in every area of our lives. The change in our minds, wills and emotions is all a direct result of the Father's Love shining and shedding glorious love in our hearts. Our hearts hold the deposit of the love of God's heart, therefore, we must empty ourselves of self-love.

God's Word, his expression of love, is what transforms and renews us, and his wisdom guides us into the Truth. We no longer look to be filled and satisfied with worldly desires, we look to the perfect law of liberty as its truth unfolds before us.

To God alone we bend our knees; we bow and break our hearts in total allegiance to our Bridegroom King. His Word spoken to us unfurls our hearts as petals in the sunlight until we are wholly open to receive what the hand of God would bring.

His hand is stretched out to us to welcome us into his embrace, and we become completely vulnerable, completely accessible to him as we step into the circle of his arms. We are lost to everything but him, his glorious face and the longing and deep desire within us to be filled with the words of his mouth. We realize if man is not to live by bread alone but every word that passes from the mouth of God, then we are desperate to receive from him, this glorious God-Man who loves us so completely with such perfection and purity.

We whisper to him, "I am wholly thine, thank you that in your mercy and love I have found redemption and forgiveness and you have turned to me, showing me by experience how gracious you are to me. Not only have you turned to me, but you have come to me. You have, by your Spirit, come into me and we are one. I am no longer my own; I have been bought by your precious blood and I have no right to let sin have dominion over me.

"It is you, Father, who I long to have dominion over me, so strengthen me, perfect me, uphold me and teach me how to be established in your Word so that no iniquity has dominion over me. Show me, as I sit before you, how to go through your Word so that I can be built up in my faith.

"I have come to recognize that all of life is a battleground and the enemy of my soul could be lurking around any corner. I need to be fit for the battle both spiritually and physically so that the eyes of my heart see the hurdles ahead and, instead of running headlong into them, I am able to leap over and continue the fight. By the power of your Word, I am able to pursue and overtake each area of resistance and not turn back. I seek to destroy these areas, no longer allowing them to have power in my life.

"You will be my light in times of darkness, my sufficiency in times of need and the joy of my heart to give me strength to overcome. Your Word in me will cause my heart to rejoice as I see the power and might of your strength over the enemies of my soul as they fall under my feet.

"I have chosen the best part of life; I have chosen to die in order to find myself in you. To find myself in you… that means I am no longer ruled by the passions and lusts of the world and my flesh, for I have put them to death. My life, my everyday normal life is hidden with Christ in God, and that means that my outward characteristics are a reflection of who you are. That means I am covered in love, but what does that look like to others?"

Child of my heart; to be covered in love is to be under my protection, for you have chosen to put on the new you who has been renewed in knowledge according to the image of who I have created you to be.

Your life is becoming and lovely and peaceful, for it is a life of holiness and joy. Your heart is tender towards others and mercy and kindness mark your way. Gentleness and compassion rise up in you when your heart becomes aware of the needs people have.

Your walk is one of humility when you choose submission with joy when a test comes your way. My peace holds you steady in the midst of the storm, and because you have ridden out the storm and experienced my comfort, you extend comfort and patience to others in their times of need.

You have been forgiven much, therefore, you are quick to forgive others. You do not carry an offense, for you keep your mind set on things above. You are consumed with loving me wholeheartedly.

My Word dwells richly within your heart and I have a resting place there. I am always at work in you to perfect and establish you so that you walk consistently according to the counsel of my will.

A life of love lived here on earth resembles Jesus, and as you grow in giving him grace to be the dominant lover, your face shall reflect his glory. As it was with Moses so shall you radiate with the glorious goodness of the Lord your God. There shall be no other loves in your life competing with mine.

In your walk with me, you have been an eager student, desiring to learn of me as I cause my Word to come forth in your life in practical ways. The practical then becomes the miraculous as you believe my promises and see them come to pass. Open your mouth and I will fill it. Feed on my faithfulness and surely you shall be fed.

 # TSADHE

Resembling a scythe or reaping hook or sickle,
main instruments used to harvest.

## PSALM 119:137–144

[137] *Righteous are You, O Lord,*
*And upright are Your judgments.*

[138] *You have commanded Your testimonies in righteousness*
*And exceeding faithfulness.*

[139] *My zeal has consumed me,*
*Because my adversaries have forgotten Your words.*

[140] *Your word is very pure,*
*Therefore Your servant loves it.*

[141] *I am small and despised,*
*Yet I do not forget Your precepts.*

[142] *Your righteousness is an everlasting righteousness,*
*And Your law is truth.*

[143] *Trouble and anguish have come upon me,*
*Yet Your commandments are my delight.*

[144] *Your testimonies are righteous forever;*
*Give me understanding that I may live.*

YOU AND I have been gathered in as part of the great end time harvest. Through God's eternal perspective he sees us as individual shafts of wheat. In his omniscience he sees each shaft in every stage of growth. He has seen the grain of wheat that has fallen to the ground and died in order to bear fruit— it is with immense pleasure and delight the Father sets and rests his gaze upon us.

He is intent upon one thing: loving us with exceeding faithfulness and perfect truth and purity. His deep desire is that we enter into union with him. To be in union with him is to have our hearts beating as one, breaking over the same things as break his. Our eyes will shed streams of tears over the unsaved because of our personal experience of the grace and mercy of God.

The law of love has ruled from life to death to life in the resurrection power of God. It is in the resurrection that we see the incredible faithfulness and utter trustworthiness of the Father, our King and our Majestic Ancient of Days. All that he has done he has commanded in righteousness and truth, and all that he has required of us is in order to bring forth righteousness, truth and purity from our inner beings.

God is watching and waiting for a harvest of souls that will become his church, and he has declared he is coming for a church, his Bride, who will be without spot or blemish. Altogether lovely we will be to him in our purity; our desire for holiness will beautify and perfect us.

Even now, he is separating the wheat from the chaff. The chaff he blows away as dust in the wind and what remains are the harvested souls before him. He bears us up as he delves into the dark corners of our souls and his touch brings forth a softening of our hardened hearts. The rigid outer shells of our hearts break as we recognize and take ownership of our sinfulness and purpose to make choices that will cause our old nature to submit to the new man that has been birthed in the likeness of Christ.

As we receive his Word into our hearts, the softness there causes an expansion. The imparted Word becomes implanted and a change is underway, a change seen by the eyes of God, who stands ready with reaping hook in hand.

He is in the harvest field and his eyes focus on each single stalk of wheat. Even in such a large expanse he is able to instantly see only you and only me. Nothing is crowding his view as he surveys the field of hearts in various stages of transformation. He knows that he has deposited within each of us the qualities of perseverance and endurance. The storms of life come upon us but our roots have grown deep into the Word of God and we, too, sense a change in our reactions.

No longer are we stiff and starchy, trying to endure with a stiff upper lip, but glory to God, there is gentleness in our hearts that gives way to kindness and goodness! As we have desired to be sensitive to the Father we have recognized the need to be diligent and disciplined, and now in our lives his will is being done and his praise is being sung.

Our lives are being lived each step in step with the Spirit, thereby walking in agreement with the Father and beginning to see the abundance of God coming forth. Fruitfulness is a direct result of the Father's pruning as he cuts away all that is not pleasing growth. Old flesh patterns, habits and attitudes must die and be cut off.

The purity of the harvest is of utmost importance to the Father. We must be willing to undergo the pain of purification, knowing that our suffering is momentary but will let us share his glory. Emptied of our old nature, we leave room for the weighty glory of God to dwell.

Put forth your whole heart in loving me so that your heart may not fail or falter; neither shall it tremble when troubles come your way. Allow your soul to rest upon the strength of my faithfulness towards you so that the fruit of joy can be borne out of your life.

When your soul is at rest there is no longer a clashing of our conflicting wills. Peace and joy walk hand in hand and they will lead you into the way of righteousness as you walk with an undivided and un-diluted heart within my kingdom. There shall be harmony within your soul; the song you sing will echo the song in my heart for you.

You shall skip, dancing with joy for you have entered into the joy of your Lord and you see your life changing all around. There becomes a clear and new dimension that you walk in as you gaze upon the beauty of my grace and keep on seeking my face.

Come freely into the circle of my embrace; dance with me as an expression of your love and joy. Dance with joyous abandon—take my hands and let me lead you in a dance of intimacy.

You are so precious to me and I long to show you my heart, my tender and compassionate heart full of unbridled love for you. You are my treasure and you bring great pleasure to me. I will never hurt you or betray your love, and in your dance with me I long for you to experience the purity of my love.

So, just come into the circle of my embrace. Let me show you that, although many have forgotten my words, their purity and truth stands forever. My wisdom is as pure as my love—it is considerate and gentle, full of compassion and good fruit.

You are protected by my compassion, for it shields you, nurtures you and brings nourishment to you. My compassion causes you to grow strong even as it breaks your heart in order to bring healing. It is always your choice as to whether or not you surrender. It is always my choice to love unconditionally and without measure.

*The joy of love will ease the pain of the cutting of the uncircumcised heart.* The joy of love will welcome the sight of me in the harvest field of hearts with my reaping hook in hand. The joy of love will cause your heart to run to me and to not shrink back so that I am able to cut away the growth that does not please me and give you greater understanding that you may live out the abundance I have laid hold of for you. Enter into the joy of Jesus and live your life making room for the glory of God to dwell within you. Make decisions that will see your flesh patterns decrease and die and then you shall see the truth of the shining glory of God within you blazing for the unsaved world to see.

 QOPH

Symbolic meaning is of behind, the last, least.
Literal meaning is 'back of the head.'

## PSALM 119:145–152

[145] *I cried with all my heart; answer me, O Lord!*
  *I will observe Your statutes.*

[146] *I cried to You; save me*
  *And I shall keep Your testimonies.*

[147] *I rise before dawn and cry for help;*
  *I wait for Your words.*

[148] *My eyes anticipate the night watches,*
  *That I may meditate on Your word.*

[149] *Hear my voice according to Your lovingkindness;*
  *Revive me, O Lord, according to Your ordinances.*

[150] *Those who follow after wickedness draw near;*
  *They are far from Your law.*

[151] *You are near, O Lord,*
  *And all Your commandments are truth.*

[152] *Of old I have known from Your testimonies*
  *That You have founded them forever.*

I WALK WITH you in companionship. You are my friend and no good thing will I withhold from those who love me.

My presence is with you at all times, and though my answer seems long in coming to you, my grace is all you need. I am able and ready to meet all of your needs, able to fulfill all of your desires. I am able and I am willing and I will reveal myself to those who seek my face, but know that, even before you see my face, I am already revealing myself.

You will see Jesus resolutely setting his face like flint to do my will and looking towards the Cross knowing life will triumph over death. He knew this because in the darkest hours of his deepest despair he found me faithful.

*I am building in you a house for holy habitation.* How well I know the weight of the glory that I long to have rest upon you in all its fullness. When you cannot see my face, then it is time to stand fast and trust my Word. And when my Word seems far from your heart, then it is time to trust the strength of my mighty right hand.

*When shall I hear the cry of your heart that echoes Paul* when he fell prostrate at my feet and cried "Who are You, Lord?" Who am I? To you, my Beloved Child—who am I?

I have called you friend, so be as at peace in our times of silence as you are when you see my hand orchestrating answers to your prayers. *Even in your darkest hours, I am Jehovah Shalom* and I change not. Listen in the silence for the sound of my steady heartbeat. You will find comfort in the silence, for it is then that you will find rest for your soul. Inner rest of the soul befits holiness, and without holiness you shall not see me.

I am the Light in your world; there is no darkness in me at all. Your life is hid in Christ—in me—and your whole body is to be full of light. Therefore, that which is darkness within you must surrender to the Light of truth. Yielded and surrendered obedience is what I am looking to see in your heart. I desire a heart with an attitude of gratitude, a heart that holds and hums my song of praise and melodious love.

*I am looking for a people* who have determined in their hearts to look to me in the darkest hours before dawn and to be willing in that time to wait in silence for me alone, even looking forward to the wakeful hours during the night in which their hearts will meditate on my Word.

And as my Word finds a resting place within your heart, I shall know that I, too, have found a welcome and a resting place. Truly, I am able to find comfort within the confines your heart.

I am training you in righteousness. As an active soldier must report for duty, so am I placing opportunities within your daily life that will test your mettle. When those times come, will you find that you have reported for duty and, in fact, followed orders well?

A part of training in righteousness is presenting yourself as a living sacrifice whose holiness is acceptable. My robe of righteousness has been given to you; yet your level of personal holiness is an area in which you grow. My blood has cleansed you of all sin and it has redeemed you from the curse of the law.

*To walk in the fullness of my blessing is to walk in surrendered obedience*, considering yourself dead to sin. Anything not of faith is sin; therefore, in the midst of your difficulty, before you see even a hint of change in your circumstances, praise me. Wait upon me, wait for me and watch for my salvation.

Have I not said that my eyes shall be upon the faithful ones in the land so that they may dwell with me? Those who walk in a blameless way are those who minister to me. Is not the thought of ministering to me in any way worth the death of sin—worth living a life of saying no to the flesh so that holiness and purity can rise up strong within you?

So, as you give heed to the blameless way, you will find me quick to come to you. Keep the walls of your heart full of integrity and set no worthless thing before your eyes. Let those things see the back of your head as you turn fully away from them. Run to me and I shall revive you by the power of my Word and even by so much as my breath upon your cheek. My glory falls in the beauty of holiness.

*Let your heart find joy in me and look forward to spending time with me. You are not bound by duty—you are bound by unbreakable cords of love.*

Let blessing and honor and praise flow from your lips even when your way is fraught with difficulty. Let praise flow out of your lips even before you see the goodness of God poured into your life. Daily present yourself before me, knowing that I have all your days written in my Book of Life. All of your activities of all your days are recorded there.

Submit yourself to my Spirit so that my plans and purposes for you are fulfilled. Yield not to the desires of your flesh, but rather, submit and surrender those to me even though they are wide open for my continual perusal. Yield them at the fiery altar so that which is flesh is burnt; the wood, hay and stubble of your life are removed; and nothing but a mound of ashes is left to be exchanged for beauty.

Remember, a diamond is fashioned out of a lump of coal and, as a skilled craftsman, I bring out the finest in the diamond by much cutting and polishing. I have a setting that will perfectly show the flawless beauty of each unique diamond. Look upon me so you might reflect my glory and let purity and holiness and the willingness to live chastely before me be your motivators for turning your back to sinful ways. Then the glory of the Lord shall be your rear guard and I shall continually guide you; my grace will enable and empower you to overcome sin and I shall bring such satisfaction and strength to you that never again shall I see the back of your head as you turn from me to submit to sin's desires.

# RESH

Literal meaning is 'front of the forehead.'
Symbolic meaning is *person, head, highest.*

## PSALM 119:153–160

*153 Look upon my affliction and rescue me,*
*For I do not forget Your law.*

*154 Plead my cause and redeem me;*
*Revive me according to Your word.*

*155 Salvation is far from the wicked,*
*For they do not seek Your statutes.*

*156 Great are Your mercies, O Lord;*
*Revive me according to Your ordinances.*

*157 Many are my persecutors and my adversaries,*
*Yet I do not turn aside from Your testimonies.*

*158 I behold the treacherous and loathe them,*
*Because they do not keep Your word.*

*159 Consider how I love Your precepts;*
*Revive me, O Lord, according to Your lovingkindness.*

*160 The sum of Your word is truth,*
*And every one of Your righteous ordinances is*
*everlasting.*

GOD THE FATHER is building his home within us, and because he desires for it to be all glorious within, he gets very up close and personal with us. He sees a palace within our hearts and he causes us to come face to face with him in order to work through issues in our hearts, leaving nothing untouched.

How often during the building of this home do we cry out for him to stop the work, thinking we can no longer bear the discomfort of the afflictions upon us? We rail against them, wanting to be rescued, and yet, we must persevere, press in and trust God, regardless of what we see in the natural.

In our times of testing and trial we must wholly turn towards God and talk intimately with him about giving up what we want to seek his purposes for our lives instead. Seeking the Father and discovering and doing his will is our primary purpose in life; therefore, let us go from remembering his word merely for the sake of our rescue to being willing to be broken on the Potter's wheel.

Our Jesus is the Potter and we are the clay. He has known us since the very beginning of time and, as formless lumps of clay, we must allow him to be intimate with us, to interact with us, not from afar, but as a Master Potter who is creating something flawless and absolutely perfect. We must allow him to touch every part of us even as a potter's hand is in contact with every molecule of the clay he is working with.

The clay, in turn, responds to the skillful touch and shaping of the Potter's hands, and in the same way we realize our resistance to the turning and the shaping will hinder only ourselves. The Potter has a plan and a purpose, and he always perfects us for he longs for his desire to be fulfilled in us.

He longs to see the beauty of holiness in our lives. He wants us to know that if we were never tested we would never know the power of God at work in us. We would never know that, regardless of what our natural eyes observe, and having our faith spurred on by love, we can totally trust him to work things for our good when we continue in our love and obedience to him.

We have persecutors and adversaries who seek the destruction of our souls, but we are experiencing daily the greatness of the mercies of God, and his Word keeps us steady and on course. Our intimacy with our Bridegroom King is what causes us to press forward towards him, straining for the prize Jesus offers.

Every one of his words has proven true. Because we love him, we have taught ourselves how to bless the Lord and been diligent to ever keep his Word before our eyes; even as the Lord commanded in Deuteronomy 6:8, we have kept them as "frontals" on our foreheads.

My heart cries, "May the fragrance of my Bridegroom King surround me, drawing me ever closer into his presence until I am nestled in his embrace of fire."

What is the practical reality of having a face to face intimate relationship with God as we live out our daily lives? We need to wake up from our slumbering state and no longer allow the enemy of our souls to numb us into living in compromise. The Word of God exhorts us, teaching us how to live rightly before the King, and if we are going to believe that the sum of his Word is truth, then we must recognize the areas of compromise and deceit that we allow to run rampant in our lives.

It is time to check these things, for with them clinging onto us we cannot enter the door marked Purity. We can talk about circumcision of the heart, but what truly happens when the covering is pulled back—what will be exposed?

Some will see anger as a sprawling weed growing virtually unchecked, while others will see the green shoots of envy discoloring their relationships and its partner jealousy trying to choke out the fruit of love. These unchecked weeds are flourishing at the altar of idolatry.

Our flesh must be trained to walk in the fruit of righteousness and we must take the sword in our hands to cut out the roots of the weeds, not allowing any shoots to remain in our hearts. Pledging allegiance to our King requires active service on our part. That means faithfully coming to him to allow his written words to wash our hearts and renew our minds.

We must allow the fingers of the Holy Spirit to reach deep within us to purge us completely. His new wine cannot be poured into old and shriveled wineskins. We must be moved from the smoke of the fire into the fire of God itself and be willing to bear the marks of affliction before we receive the blessing.

Our souls must become faint with longing for the salvation of our God.

It is at our point of weariness that Grace takes over. Hope rises as the wisdom of Grace's lessons are revealed, and maturity causes the eyes of our hearts to see more clearly as we behold the beauty of his Majesty.

Ever endeavor to keep your time spent with me as the highest and truest priority in your life. Only as you are still in your soul can you truly hear my voice. That is why I have given you peace to be your maidservant. Peace serves you by bringing my word from your heart to the forefront of your mind. Peace will help you and minister to you in the midst of affliction. Peace will help capture the little foxes that tend to run unchecked in your life. Peace will faithfully guard your heart. Peace will be a reflection of my heart towards you in all things, so extend grace that peace may rule.

In order for you, my child, to walk victoriously in a dark and darkening hour, you need me more than ever before to guide you through the treachery of the times at hand.

Just when you think you've got it, when the light of revelation shines in your heart and illuminates the false thinking in your mind, there is more to come. There is much more, so let your strength be found in the humility and grace of Jesus.

Always let grace condition your heart. As you learn to walk under grace's authority, I will anoint your eyes so you can clearly see the snares of the enemy. Wisdom shall guide you so you no longer fall into the nets that are set to trap you. With quickness, the authority of your Master shall be upon your lips and you will declare the wonders of my salvation. Grace will deliver you from sin and grace will empower you to rise on eagle's wings and soar above natural circumstances. Grace will cause you to love, for my grace extended to you is far stronger than your own determination.

Determine only, like Jesus, to set your face like flint to do my will, and then know that it is by my mercies that we meet and I see you at the cross, washed in my blood.

I see you seated here with me in heavenly places and my glory is resplendent upon you. Be confident of my presence with you in your coming and going. Allow me, your head and your leader in love, to have the highest place in your heart. Let my words roll around in your mind throughout your days and hear the whisper of my voice in the stillness of your nights.

Rise up each morning refreshed and encouraged in your spirit, knowing you are being renewed day after day as you grow in the grace and knowledge of who I am to you. You are forever my Beloved; forever I carry you within me.

As the womb of the mother protects and nourishes the child she is carrying, so daily, moment by moment, I cover you, whom I have formed as the precious, pure apple of my eye and sheer delight of my heart. I carry you in my womb and I am watching over you, seeing the image of Christ being formed in you daily. The Holy Spirit flows from me to you, infusing you with strength and filling you with rivers of living water. My blood protects you and nothing can overcome the power of my blood at work in your life. Nothing can overcome the power of my blood at work in you.

 # SHIN

Shin represents 'a chewing tooth' or
teeth that consume and destroy.

## PSALM 119:161–168

[161] *Princes persecute me without cause,*
*But my heart stands in awe of Your words.*

[162] *I rejoice at Your word,*
*As one who finds great spoil.*

[163] *I hate and despise falsehood,*
*But I love Your law.*

[164] *Seven times a day I praise You,*
*Because of Your righteous ordinances.*

[165] *Those who love Your law have great peace,*
*And nothing causes them to stumble.*

[166] *I hope for Your salvation, O Lord,*
*And do Your commandments.*

[167] *My soul keeps Your testimonies,*
*And I love them exceedingly.*

[168] *I keep Your precepts and Your testimonies,*
*For all my ways are before You.*

WHAT WE "CHEW OVER" in our minds is directly related to what our hearts delight in. What we "chew over" in our minds also determines the amount of glory that shines through our lives. Jesus told us that a man's words come forth from the abundance in his heart, for as we think in our hearts so are we.

When the twelve spies went out to check out the Promised Land, ten of them reported back, revealing, above all else, how they felt about themselves. Did they believe that they were the sought-after lovers of Almighty God? In the midst of the miraculous did their hearts sing with joy for knowing by experience the extraordinary provisions of an intimate and holy God whose eye was upon them with love and mercy? His hand was ever showing them kindness—a kindness, if they would allow it, that could break their hearts so that they would be wholly his.

The Lord God did not see them as grasshoppers. In his eyes they were sons of the King; strength, might and valor belonged to them and victory was sure because of his promise.

Today this remains the same: the sum of his Word is truth—if we add up all the words of God, truth will forever be the balance of the equation. Have we been disciplined soldiers reporting to the Commander in Chief? Have we sought after his commands in order to fully carry out his orders? When princes come to persecute us, we can stand steady, ready for the ensuing battle, for we have heard him speak.

We move ourselves into a place of victory whenever we choose to enter his chambers and incline our hearts to hear his Word. He always leads us in triumph throughout the time of battle. Even though the victory may be slow in appearing, we do not need to grow weary and lose heart and hope.

One thing is sure—this day, this moment of time can never be relived. It may be replayed in our minds, but it can never be changed.

When our hearts delight and find joy in the Father's Word, we have strength from heaven to stand in awe of him as we see the internal changes he is bringing forth. Heavenly strength, a gift of deep joy, keeps us standing firm as we walk with him in steadfastness, purposing to obey with love. As we settle all our hopes upon him and him alone, hope, grace and obedience underscore our minds.

One thing we desire, one thing we truly long for: to behold the beauty of our Lord and to be enveloped in his fragrance and beauty. We can make choices that flaunt the efforts of self, but for victorious living we must choose to let go of fleshly endeavors and cling to the Word of God, which brings grace and truth into our daily lives.

Grace enables us to do the unseen, gives us great peace and keeps us from stumbling. Our hope for the salvation of the Lord is answered in the promises of God, and on these we meditate, chewing them over in our minds so that we find ourselves keeping and walking in the precepts and principles of Heaven's Ruler.

The glory and light of the Lord illuminates our illusions and all falsehood in our inner lives is dropped. Love is the impetus of our obedience, love spurs us to hope and love excels in grace and mercy given.

"I am love," he gently says as he stoops down to soothe my furrowed brow.

I am love and with love do I see all of your ways, understanding all of your whys, seeing and knowing the hidden reasons of your heart.

I see the good, the best and the highest, for that is the direction I am looking. The hidden motives of your heart are cloaked with love and I want to shout your victory from the mountain heights and erase from your memory the taunts of the enemy.

You are standing in the palace of the King. I see you standing with such grace and beauty, for you are glorious within. The gold interwoven in your clothing shimmers as it reflects the glory of the God you are beholding. Golden glory light is your cloak and the awareness of my presence ever near has influenced your thought life.

You have recognized yourself early on as a pauper and a beggar, and behold! I have given you the Kingdom. You have mourned over your sinfulness, interceded for others as you have felt their pain and you have known my comfort—your soul has known my consolations. With gentle heart and humble spirit you have trusted and obeyed me. All that I have, I give to you.

Freely you have received and freely and faithfully you have been giving. You have hungered a deep, heart-wrenching hunger for me and felt as empty as a dried-up well, but as I have showed you my righteousness, each glance, each longing look has been enough to fill the wellsprings of your heart with the water of Life that never shall run dry.

You have shared your meat and drink with others; many souls have been strengthened by the food from your outstretched hand. Always, in your longing my faithfulness has seen that you are fed.

*Even the cup of sorrowing and suffering which you have had to partake of has quenched your thirst and yet left you wanting more, for you have learned that Suffering and Glory walk together.* One cannot be had without the other. Suffering has taught you the necessity of mercy—mercy given and mercy received. Mercy is compassion and love in action, bringing to fruition that dream for you that I, for eternity, have cherished and treasured in my heart for you.

*As a child loses its baby teeth, growing molars and larger teeth to chew with, so you have experienced the losses and pains of growth. I have watched and waited as you have encountered* times of hardship and indecision, and you have always placed in my hands that which your mind has struggled with. You found rest for your soul as you ceased from your own laboring and simply trusted in my Word and my Faithfulness. My Word has given you much to provoke your mind and change your heart. Your course of direction has altered as you have chosen to move closer and be aligned with Truth.

For how else can we be one, save for the choices of your heart and soul to die so that I may live in and through you? How else can we be one, save that you be willing to die that you might live in me, a triumphant, victorious warrior with a girdle of gold about your breast. Joined in death, we live exultantly, expectantly.

The qualities of your heart will be interwoven with gold because you have been in the Refiner's Fire and have the glory of the Lord God upon you. Always remember that though you be in the midst of the fire, there you are in the midst of me, for I Am a consuming fire. You are in the center of my heart and it is burning with passionate love for you. In the consummation of the fire we become one in death and life.

**TAV**

Symbolic meaning is "Covenant, to seal."
Literal meaning is 'sign, cross.'
Tav would be our signature or closing mark in life.

## PSALM 119:169–176

<sup>169</sup> *Let my cry come before You, O Lord;*
*Give me understanding according to Your word.*

<sup>170</sup> *Let my supplication come before You;*
*Deliver me according to Your word.*

<sup>171</sup> *Let my lips utter praise,*
*For You teach me Your statutes.*

<sup>172</sup> *Let my tongue sing of Your word,*
*For all Your commandments are righteousness.*

<sup>173</sup> *Let Your hand be ready to help me,*
*For I have chosen Your precepts.*

<sup>174</sup> *I long for Your salvation, O Lord,*
*And Your law is my delight.*

<sup>175</sup> *Let my soul live that it may praise You,*
*And let Your ordinances help me.*

<sup>176</sup> *I have gone astray like a lost sheep; seek Your servant,*
*For I do not forget Your commandments.*

THE END HAS come. We are at the last line, the last page of the letter, and how we have lived will determine the flourish of our signature.

Our lives have been letters from our Lord Jesus Christ and upon our hearts have been written the words of God.

Many have read the letters of our lives and been changed and challenged, but have we read our own mail and conformed freely and joyously to the contents therein? The hand of love has written every word and our own lives have been marked by the power of God's Word. It has always been Jesus our God-Man-Companion-Lover who has made all the difference in how our lives have been played out.

We have fed on his faithfulness, chewed his Word in the core of our beings and seen transformation take place in our minds. Our ears have heard his Voice tenderly directing us, and we have followed his way and borne the good fruit of that decision in our lives. He has spoken words of courage to us in our times of tumult and our hearts have been strengthened. The resolve and desire to do only his will and to walk in the way he has prepared for us has lifted us to a higher level of intimacy with him. Joy in him has been our greatest delight.

Time after time, we have experienced and entered into the rejoicing of his heart, knowing we are the apple of his eye, the recipients of his amazing love.

How could it be any other way but that our heart-cry would always be heard and understood by he who gave his very life that we might live forever with him? How could it be any other way but that we would cry out in yearning for a deep understanding of his Word, his very Heart, and then cry out some more? How could it be any other way but that a song of joyous praise and adoration would be upon our lips for the daily deliverance his Word has brought to every aspect of our lives?

In his great patience he has taught us tenderly, instructing us in his laws and statutes, and we have learned to order our lives by them, teaching our spirits to be ruled by the Holy Spirit.

He watches over us and nurtures us with compassion, ever seeing the seed of understanding growing meat upon its bones. The growth of understanding forms a new man inside with a heart always eager to be taught the Word and a tongue ready with a Song of the Sword. Praise is upon the lips of the man who has allowed the Names of God to be written across the hallmarks of his life. Continual hope in God brings him deep joy and disappointment is far from him.

Along our journey we have entered many crucibles that have purified us and caused us to come forth as refined silver. It is said about us that our character is sterling and we are found faithful and trustworthy. We have not drawn back but have wholeheartedly embraced the glory of his purging, cleansing fire.

We stand at the door; it is the burning fiery love of Jesus we are entering into and the beauty of the blaze births in us a passion for surrender.

We carry the treasure of the Glory of God in our earthly vessels. We are vessels that are weak and broken and yet, with unmitigated strength, we abide in the shelter the high and holy God offers to us underneath the shadow of his wings. As we abide there we will be able to rest under the weight of his glory.

For it is as we are in the presence of holiness that we become so. We are like chameleons in the world, but to God, all of who we are is laid bare. The truth of who we are reveals itself to us as we hear the voice of God tenderly speaking to our hearts.

As every moment of every day of our lives is lived in the light of his holy purity, our conscious thoughts are more apt to be God–focused and God-centered, and ultimately our subconscious thoughts take care of themselves. That which is underneath receives a constant cleansing as we renew our minds with the Word of God. Like a magnet to metal and a moth to the flame we are inexplicably drawn to the center of our Father's heart.

Holy purity is seen in the lives of those who are wholly consecrated and set apart for the glory of God, those who have emptied their lives of self's desires—not just for God's praise for works well done, but in order to be full of something much greater. How can we carry the weighty worthiness and honorableness of God Almighty in anything less than sanctified lives?

To be reflective is to meditate, and a reflective life is a translucent life in which the purity and clarity of God is clearly seen. As we reflect on him and his Word and enjoy the company of his presence, unbeknownst to us, his light, which bursts forth from the depths of his being and shines brighter than the noonday sun, will also shine through us.

To love God is to practice obeying his admonitions, to meditate upon his Word day and night, to hunger and thirst for the truths found in his Word more than our necessary food and water, to pant after him even as a deer pants for water.

Will I die so that he may live through me? Will I die to my will, my way, my wantonness? Will I let his glory bring light to my understanding so that I might know how to put on the newness of truth in my mind and how to walk and live and talk like God in true righteousness and holiness. The breastplate of righteousness guards the glory of God within me even as it breaks the power of sin's dominion over me by my consistent good and right choices enabling me to walk in the love and peace of God.

# BECKONED
## BY THE KING

IN OUR DARKNESS and weakness, the Father woos us with his light and love, infusing strength and grace into the lives of his children. He invites each one of us to journey further with him in order to touch the deepest core of his heart. We answer his beckoning to press closer to him and tarry with him, and thus we learn to walk as kings and priests unto our God.

We spend so much of our time hoping that we are someone of worth whose life matters, wanting to know that what we have and what we do counts. In the natural we strive and are restless; peace eludes us, discontent settles in and soon we feel lost.

What we need is the knowledge that the "whosoever" and "the whole world" have been narrowed down to you and to me, and this knowledge can only be gained by experiencing the Father's deep and tender love for us. We need to know that the worth we are to the Father is infinite and far beyond our ability to grasp, yet ours to live in and find rest and shelter in.

We need to learn that the riches of the inheritance of the saints belongs to us. Jesus became poor so that we could become rich. He poured out his mercy and emptied himself of all that was good and perfect and holy so that we could partake of his fullness. We are eternally joined with the King of Kings and he delights in richly lavishing us with every good thing to enjoy.

Our response is to live our lives displaying the virtues and righteousness of God that Jesus has made available to us. We align ourselves with the Word of truth and allow the Spirit of truth to renew our minds and create in us the desire to follow the path of the Cross. We decide to die to self so that the new man inside of us can rise up and live each day in the power of God. We practice stillness so that we know our God and can recognize his Voice as clearly in times of tumult as we do in the stillness of our quiet time.

As sons and daughters of the King, we are fully equipped to carry out the plans and purposes God holds in his heart for us. We are people of rich love, great peace and full joy— lacking nothing. He holds out to each of us this true life that is found and revealed hidden in Christ.

So much of life is hindered because we fear our circumstances; however, it is in taking the first step outside of our boundaries of fear that we are able to experience the sufficiency of God. Our lives then become characterized by freedom, peace and joy as we are strengthened by the courage we gain by trusting God and finding him faithful.

May each reader answer the beckoning of the King and walk free in the power of his love.

# About the Author

Jeannie lives in Hanna, Alberta, Canada, and her greatest desire is to apprehend and be apprehended by the love of God. She encourages others to pursue a deeper walk of faith by bringing the Word to life in practical ways, forgetting those things which are behind and reaching forward to those things which are ahead, hidden in Christ. Her longing is to be known as a friend of God, walking a walk of steadfast love, humility and service towards others.

Printed in the United States
111001LV00001B/151-249/P

9 781897 373170